ESSENTIAL REPERTOIRE

FOR THE YOUNG CHOIR

BY
JANICE KILLIAN
MICHAEL O'HERN
LINDA RANN
EDITED BY
EMILY CROCKER

ISBN 978-0-7935-4335-9

HAL•LEONARD® CORPORATION

7777 W. BLUEMOUND RD. P.O. BOX 13819 MILWAUKEE, WI 53213

AUTHORS

Dr. Janice Killian, Music Education
Texas Woman's University, Denton, Texas

Michael O'Hern, Choral Director
Lake Highlands Junior High
Richardson Independent School District, Texas

Linda Rann, Choral Director
Dan F. Long Middle School
Carrollton-Farmers Branch Independent School
District, Texas

PROJECT EDITOR
Emily Crocker
Director of Choral Publications
Hal Leonard Corporation, Milwaukee, Wisconsin

PRODUCTION EDITOR
Ryan French
Choral Editor
Hal Leonard Corporation, Milwaukee, Wisconsin

CONSULTANTS
Glenda Casey, Choral Director
Berkner High School
Richardson Independent School District, Texas

Bobbie Douglass, Choral Director
L. D. Bell High School
Hurst-Euless-Bedford Independent School District,
Texas

Jan Juneau, Choral Director
Klein High School
Klein Independent School District, Texas

Dr. John Leavitt, Composer and Conductor
Wichita, Kansas

Brad White, Choral Director
Richland High School
Birdville Independent School District, Texas

Send all inquiries to:
Hal Leonard Corporation
7777 W. Bluemound Rd., Box 13819
Milwaukee, WI 53213

CONTENTS

CONTENTS cont.

 # TO THE TEACHER

Why We Wrote This Book

We created this series because we are vitally committed to the nurturing of choral music, to the more effective teaching of choral music, and particularly to the encouragement of the young musicians who perform choral music. We believe that every child is musically expressive and deserves the opportunity to explore that capacity.

Too often, our definitions of literacy have been limited to words on paper. Although aspects of music can be taught as the written word (i.e., as a series of facts or as a written symbolic language), ultimately music is best understood not through the written word, but rather as a unique way of looking at the world, a special dimension of human understanding. What one understands, expresses, or feels when performing choral music is indeed "another way of knowing." We believe that it is vital that our children be given opportunities to experience this expanded literacy.

Janice Killian   **Michael O'Hern**   **Linda Rann**

About the Series

The four levels of *Essential Repertoire* (Young Choir, Developing Choir, Concert Choir, and Concert Choir - Artist Level) contain choral literature especially selected for choirs of differing ages and experience levels.

Level I, *Essential Repertoire for the Young Choir*, contains selections which take into account the limitations of the early adolescent voice. It contains musically accessible pieces which would be ideal for the beginning of the year, as well as selections appropriate for later in the year, or for groups which are ready for a special challenge. *Essential Repertoire for the Young Choir* is specifically designed for seventh and eighth graders, but the material included might be appropriate for any chorus, regardless of age.

Features of the Program

Each repertoire book contains a wide range of literature:

- a variety of historical periods
- a variety of other countries and cultures
- a mixture of English and foreign-language texts
- a variety of challenging and beginning level songs
- mixture of styles: masterworks, folksongs and spirituals; a cappella and accompanied pieces; sacred and secular works; arrangements of familiar songs; and a few pop-style selections

Every effort was made to select high quality, time-tested literature.

Each song is independent of the others, i.e. there is no special sequence intended. Little prior knowledge is assumed on the part of the student. Teachers are encouraged to make selections as needed to create a varied and meaningful classroom and concert program.

Student information pages are included with each choral selection to help students learn basic musical skills, to discover to the cultural context in which the music was created, and to evaluate their own progress.

The Teacher Editions contain the same information as the student text, plus much additional background information, as well as suggested lesson plans, vocal warm-ups, and performance tips.

The repertoire books are designed to be used in conjunction with *Essential Musicianship*, Book 1, a comprehensive choral method for teaching vocal technique, sight-singing, and music theory.

How to Use *Essential Repertoire for the Young Choir*

Each song is treated as an independent unit of study. Prior to each song is a page of information designed to be read by the student. Student pages consist of:

- Title and Composer, text information, and voicing/instrumentation.
- Cultural context of the song: Usually students can read and understand this section with limited guidance from the teacher.
- Musical terms: Students should be encouraged to find the listed terms in the song, and look up any unknown terms and/or symbols in the glossary.
- Preparation: Students will usually need teacher assistance in completing the Preparation section. This book is not designed to be student self-paced. Additional teaching suggestions, background information, and performance tips are included in the Teacher Edition.
- Evaluation: In most cases the Evaluation section is to be completed after the notes and rhythms of the piece have been mastered. Details for guiding the students' evaluation appear in the Teacher Edition.

Students should be encouraged to read the Cultural Context and Musical Terms sections of the text page prior to learning the song. This could be an effective activity for students while the teacher is involved in taking roll or other tasks. Students will usually need assistance in completing the rest of the text page.

The Teacher Edition

The Teacher Edition includes an extensive lesson plan for each choral selection which may be taught as suggested, expanded over a six-week period, or modified as needed. Each teaching plan contains the following:

- Student Text Page (slightly reduced in size)
- Ranges and song information (key, meter, form, performance possibilities)
- Learning objectives (Essential Elements) for each song correlated with the National Standards for Arts Education
- Historical/stylistic guidelines
- Answers to any student page questions
- Vocal technique/warm-ups/exercises
- Rehearsal guidelines and notes: 1) Suggested teaching sequence, and 2) Performance tips
- Evaluation suggestions for assessing student progress on the stated objectives
- Extension ideas

Who Should Use This Book

The authors of this text, all currently-practicing choral educators, bring a combined total of more than fifty years experience to the writing of this text. Their careful suggestions of tried and proven techniques provide a valuable resource of choral ideas for polishing performances.

Choral directors who are just entering the profession are encouraged to follow the suggested teaching sequence as written for each song to gain practical teaching skills.

Experienced choral directors may want to refer to the performance tips as a source of ideas for approaching a piece and refining it.

The warmups, vocalises, or polishing exercises included for every song in the Teacher Edition are particularly applicable to a given song. They also contain a wealth of ideas and suggestions which may be applied to other choral situations.

In Conclusion

Essential Repertoire for the Young Choir, when combined with the companion volume *Essential Musicianship*, is in essence, a complete curriculum for the choral experience — a core library of repertoire aimed at awakening the singer's potential for self development, musical expression, and personal esteem.

EFFECTIVE TEACHING CHECKLIST

Preparation:

- Good planning leads to a successful rehearsal.
- Establish high expectations from the start – students want to succeed.
- Establish a routine and basic standards of behavior – and stick to it!
- Follow your planned routine every rehearsal (e.g. opening cue that rehearsal has begun, warm-up, sight-reading, repertoire, evaluation). Younger choirs, in particular, respond well to structure in a rehearsal.
- Plan, plan, plan.
- Develop long-range planning (the entire year's goals and activities, the semester, the month) and short-range planning (weekly plans and the daily lesson as they fit within the entire year's goals).
- Vary teaching strategies: modeling, peer coaching, large group, small group, cooperative learning, individual instruction, student conductors, independent practice.
- Study the score well. Anticipate problem areas.
- Be able to sing any one part while playing another.
- Know the vocal ranges of each member of the chorus.
- Select appropriate music to fit those vocal ranges.
- Remember: Out-of-range results in out-of-tune singing.
- Select music of appropriate difficulty for the group.
- Plan evaluation techniques in advance.
- Have all necessary supplies and equipment ready (music in folders or ready to pass out, tapes cued, director's folder handy, recording equipment set, etc.) before the lesson begins.
- Plan to make beautiful music at least once during every rehearsal.

Presentation:

- Begin each lesson with aural activities (singing) rather than verbal activities (talking)
- Make all parts of the lesson musical – including warm-ups and sight-reading.
- Rehearse a cappella. Use the piano as little as possible.
- Remember: Delivering information is not necessarily teaching.
- Display a positive attitude.
- Communicate effectively and concisely.
- Enthusiasm is essential.
- Make learning an enjoyable experience.
- Respect legitimate effort on the part of every student.
- Be the best musician you can be.
- Laugh often.

Pacing:

- Be mentally thirty seconds ahead of the class at all times.
- Know where the lesson will lead before it happens.
- Vary activities and standing/sitting positions.
- Plan a smooth transition from one activity to the next.
- Avoid "lag" time.
- If a "teachable" moment occurs, make the most of it.
- Avoid belaboring any one exercise, phrase, activity – come back to it at another time.
- Always give students a reason for repeating a section.
- Provide at least one successful musical experience in every rehearsal.

Evaluation:

- Assess student learning in every lesson (formally or informally).
- Vary the assessment activities.
- Consider evaluating individual as well as group effort.
- Tape the rehearsals often (audio and/or video).
- Study the rehearsal tapes: 1) to discover where overlooked errors occur, 2) to assist in planning the next rehearsal, or 3) to share findings with the students.
- Provide students with opportunities to evaluate themselves.
- Teach critical listening to the students by asking specific students or a group of students to listen for a specific thing (balance of parts in the polyphonic section, a correct uniform vowel sound on a particular word or words, rise and fall of phrase, etc.).
- Constantly evaluate what's really happening. (We often hear what we want to hear!)
- Listen, listen, listen!

NATIONAL STANDARDS FOR ARTS EDUCATION
CHORAL PERFORMING GROUPS Grades 7-8
Essential Elements for Choir

The *National Standards for Arts Education* were developed by the Consortium of National Arts Education Associations under the guidance of the National Committee for Standards in the Arts. The Standards were prepared under a grant from the U. S. Department of Education, the National Endowment for the Arts, and the National Endowment for the Humanities.

Essential Musicianship, and the corresponding repertoire collections, *Essential Repertoire for the Young Choir (Mixed, Treble, Tenor Bass)*, are a part of the series *Essential Elements For Choir* and are based on these National Standards. In order to help teachers and students attain the National Standards, the authors of *Essential Elements For Choir* have developed related statements, more specific objectives, called *Essential Elements*.

By structuring this course of study around these Essential Elements and the corresponding National Standards, teachers and their students may begin to construct a vital relationship with the arts, and in so doing, as with any subject, approach this curriculum with discipline and study. The National Standards spell out what every young American should know about the arts, and the Essential Elements provide a framework for achieving these goals.

In the chart below, the National Standards (both *Content Standards* and *Achievement Standards*) are listed in **bold italic** typeface. The corresponding Essential Elements which are used in *Essential Musicianship* and *Essential Repertoire for the Young Choir* follow each National Standard in standard typeface. Throughout the text, each specific Essential Element is identified with the corresponding National Standard, i.e. *The student will sing with tall, uniform vowels (NS 1A).*

1. SINGING ALONE AND WITH OTHERS, A VARIED REPERTOIRE OF MUSIC
A. Students sing accurately and with good breath control throughout their singing ranges, alone and in small and large ensembles.

(1) Understand the vocal mechanism including parts and functions, and the changing voice
- The student will describe and demonstrate the posture, breathing, vowel placement, and articulation necessary for good singing tone.
- The student will develop an understanding of the vocal mechanism.
- The student will develop an understanding of the breathing mechanism.
- The student will build a repertoire of effective vocalises.

(2) Develop and use correct singing posture
- The student will describe and demonstrate good posture for singing.
- The student will develop the posture and breath control needed to support choral tone through sustained phrases.

(3) Develop and use correct breathing skills
- The student will develop the diaphragmatic breathing needed to support choral tone.
- The student will develop breathing techniques emphasizing the open throat.
- The student will develop breath control adequate for performing melismas, crescendos, and supporting sustained phrases.

(4) Develop good vocal tone, demonstrating proper breath support, vowel pronunciation, and placement/focus and head/chest voice
- The student will discuss and demonstrate head and chest voice.
- The student will discuss and demonstrate correct vowel pronunciation and tone placement.
- The student will develop the posture and breath control adequate for performing melismas, crescendos, and supporting sustained phrases.

(5) Develop proper diction through correct use of vowel shapes, syllabic stress, consonants, and diphthongs
  - The student will sing with tall uniform vowels.
  - The student will develop proper diction through the use of correct vowel shapes.
  - The student will discuss and demonstrate the neutral vowel (schwa).
  - The student will discuss and demonstrate the appropriate pronunciation of diphthongs.
  - The student will develop good diction through the precise articulation of consonants.
  - The student will articulate the "r" consonant correctly.
  - The student will develop clear diction to convey the meaning of the text.

(6) Develop intonation awareness
  - The student will aurally discriminate between in-tune and out-of-tune singing.
  - The student will practice good intonation.
  - The student will develop intonation awareness through the study of whole steps and half steps.
  - The student will develop intonation awareness through the study of the chromatic scale.

(7) Exercise responsible use and care of the voice
  - The student will develop technical singing skill focusing on the responsible use and care of the voice.
  - The student will develop an appreciation of the care needed for responsible use of the voice.

B. Students sing with expression and technical accuracy a repertoire of vocal literature with a level of difficulty of 2 on a scale of 1-6 including some songs performed from memory.
(National Standard 1B applies only to non-performing groups.)

C. Students sing music representing diverse genres and cultures with expression appropriate for the work being performed.
  - The student will develop proper Latin, French, German, Catalan, Hebrew, Italian, Spanish, and English diction through the correct use of vowel shapes and syllabic stress.
  - The student will sing choral literature from Africa, Italy, France, Germany, Spain, Mexico, Israel, England, Ireland, Russia, Scotland, and the United States.
  - The student will sing choral literature of various styles including spirituals, lullabies, folk songs from around the world, jazz, pop, and gospel, as well as traditional choral literature.
  - The student will sing choral literature from various time periods including Renaissance, Baroque, Classical, Romantic, and the Twentieth Century.

D. Students sing music written in two and three parts.
  - Students will sing choral literature written for unison, two-part, three-part, and four-part choruses.

E. Students sing with expression and technical accuracy a varied repertoire of vocal literature with a level of difficulty of 3, on a scale of 1-6, including some songs performed from memory.
(National Standard 1E applies to performing groups.)
<u>Performance Activities</u>
(1) The student will perform individually, in small ensembles, and in large groups
  - The student will apply music reading skills to the performance of short accompanied or a cappella songs.
  - The student will perform in small ensembles for the choir, and where appropriate, for a wider audience.
  - The student will have the opportunity to perform solos, if desired.

(2) Articulating and practicing proper concert etiquette
  - The student will describe and demonstrate proper concert etiquette.

(3) Performance literature
  - The student will perform choral literature identified by such state and national organizations as the American Choral Directors Association, Music Educators National Conference, the Texas University Interscholastic League, the New York State School Music Association, the Wisconsin Music Educators Association, and others, as being of appropriate quality and difficulty for this age group.
<u>Choral Ensemble Techniques</u>

(4) Sing in tune through tone-vowel placement and careful listening
- The student will increase his/her ability to sing in tune while singing harmony.
- The student will improve intonation through the use of blended, supported vowels.
- The student will listen carefully to rehearsal recordings, identifying areas of intonation weaknesses.

(5) Blend with other ensemble voices in areas of tone quality, diction, and intonation
- The student will demonstrate the ability to blend with other ensemble voices utilizing appropriate tone quality, diction, and intonation.
- The student will listen carefully to rehearsal recordings, identifying areas in which blend needs improvement.

(6) Respond to conducting
- The student will respond appropriately to conducting.
- The student will view rehearsal videotapes, noticing areas in which all ensemble members are not responding to conducting gestures.

(7) Pitch and rhythm accuracy
- The student will develop rhythmic accuracy by dividing the beat.
- The student will hold long notes for full value.
- The student will perform rhythms, syncopated rhythms, and changing meters with understanding and accuracy.
- The student will aurally identify areas in which pitch accuracy needs improvement and will attempt to repair those sections of music.
- The student will develop pitch accuracy over time through repeated practice.

(8) Demonstrate style characteristics (historical period, culture, dynamics, composer intent)
- The student will perform dynamic and tempo changes as indicated by the composer.
- The student will develop choral performance techniques of the Renaissance, Baroque, Classical, Romantic, and Twentieth Century eras.
- The student will become familiar with the musical terms which appear in each of the songs studied.

(9) Demonstrate phrasing (shape, movement)
- The student will aurally discriminate between musical and unmusical phrases.
- The student will develop the ability to musically shape a phrase.
- The student will demonstrate the ability to sing long sustained phrases while maintaining pitch accuracy.

(10) Demonstrate textual clarity (word accent, syllabic stress)
- The student will aurally discriminate between appropriate and inappropriate word stress.
- The student will demonstrate the ability to sing with appropriate syllabic stress.

(11) Demonstrate expression (sensitivity, mood, physical indication of feeling)
- The student will sing expressively as indicated by appropriate facial expression.
- The student will physically express sensitivity to the text.
- The student will verbalize the meaning of the text.

2. PERFORMING ON INSTRUMENTS, ALONE AND WITH OTHERS, A VARIED REPERTOIRE OF MUSIC

It is the purpose of this course in choral performance to emphasize the development of the voice and the choral art. Therefore, instrumental performance is beyond the scope of this text. It should be noted, however, that skill on a musical instrument, particularly a keyboard, is a definite asset for a singer/chorister and such skill should be encouraged at every opportunity. Choral directors should consider such choral and instrumental combinations as:
- Using student pianists as rehearsal and/or performance accompanists.
- Using instrumental accompaniments played by students.
- Highlighting instrumentalists from within the chorus on appropriate programs.
- Arranging joint band/orchestra/choir performances whenever possible.

3. IMPROVISING MELODIES, VARIATIONS, AND ACCOMPANIMENTS
A. Students improvise simple harmonic accompaniments.
   (1) The student will improvise a harmonic accompaniment to the reading of a specified poem using an autoharp or other chordal instrument.
   (2) The student will accompany an ensemble on guitar, autoharp or keyboard.

B. Students improvise melodic embellishments and simple rhythmic and melodic variations on given pentatonic melodies and melodies in major keys.
   (1) The student will improvise short melodies in C pentatonic on Orff instruments.
   (2) The student will improvise a pentatonic piece with contrasting sections.
   (3) The student will improvise pentatonic melodies using deliberate dynamic contrasts.

C. Students improvise short melodies, unaccompanied, and over given rhythmic accompaniments, each in a consistent style, meter, and tonality.
   (1) The student will improvise short melodies over rhythmic patterns played on classroom instruments.
   (2) The student will improvise on a given syncopated rhythmic pattern.

4. COMPOSING AND ARRANGING MUSIC WITHIN SPECIFIED GUIDELINES
A. Students compose short pieces within specified guidelines, demonstrating how the elements of music are used to achieve unity and variety, tension and release, and balance.
   (1) The student will compose rhythm exercises of quarter, half, and whole note patterns.
   (2) The student will compose a short composition in 2/4, 3/4, or 4/4 meter.
   (3) The student will create a musical composition using contrasting sections.
   (4) The student will compose and perform a rhythm piece.

B. Students arrange simple pieces for voices or instruments other than those for which the pieces were written.
   (1) The student will arrange a nursery rhyme or other familiar poem for speech chorus.
   (2) The student will compose a rhythmic setting for a tongue twister and arrange it for speech chorus and classroom instruments.
   (3) The student will arrange familiar folk or patriotic songs into a medley.
   (4) The student will arrange a familiar song in a contrasting style (e.g. from traditional to swing style).

C. Students use a variety of traditional and nontraditional sound sources and electronic media when composing and arranging.
   (1) The student will use music notation softward to notate a C major scale.
   (2) Students will create musical compositions on poetry by [Robert Lewis Stevenson] using computer generated sound or other musical sources.
   (3) Students will compose brief compositions using sounds available in the classroom.

5. READING AND NOTATING MUSIC
A. Students will read whole, half, quarter, eighth, sixteenth, and dotted notes and rests in 2/4, 3/4, 4/4, 6/8, 3/8, and alle breve meter signatures.
   (1) Read, write and perform rhythm patterns
   • The student will discriminate between beat and rhythm.
   • The student will echo-sing/chant/clap rhythmic patterns.
   • The student will read and perform quarter, half, whole, eighth note, and rest rhythms accurately.
   • The student will write quarter, half, whole, eighth note, and rest rhythms accurately.
   • The student will read and perform rhythm patterns in various meters.
   • The student will read and perform rhythms in changing meter.

B. Students read at sight simple melodies in both the treble and bass clefs.
   (1) Read and sing melodic patterns and harmonic structures in a variety of keys and tonalities, using specific methodology such as solfege or numbers
   • The student will read and sing rhythmic and melodic patterns in treble and bass clefs.
   • The student will read chord patterns in the keys of C, F, and G major in treble and bass clefs.
   • The student will read and sing melodic patterns using the tonic, dominant, and subdominant chords in treble and bass clefs.
   • The student will apply knowledge of whole and half steps.

C. Students identify and define standard notation symbols for pitch, rhythm, dynamics, tempo, articulation, and expression.

(1) Demonstrate knowledge of music theory including conventional and unconventional notation
- The student will recognize and apply basic rhythmic notation (whole, half, quarter, eighth, and dotted notes and rests).
- The student will recognize and apply knowledge of basic pitch notation (grand staff, pitch names, clefs, sharps, flats, and naturals).
- The student will recognize and apply key signatures.

(2) Demonstrate knowledge of music theory by using music terminology
- The student will become familiar with the musical terms found in specific songs included in the student texts.
- The student will perform a piece of music utilizing the musical terminology indicated in the music to interpret the piece as suggested by the composer.

D. Students use standard notation to record their musical ideas and the musical ideas of others.

(1) Learn and use grandstaff, key and time signatures, pitch and rhythm notation
- The student will describe and review elements of musical notation.
- The student will recognize and apply basic rhythmic notation (whole, half, quarter, eighth, and dotted rhythms and rests).
- The student will recognize and apply basic pitch notation (grand staff, pitch names, clefs, sharp, flat and natural).
- The student will define pitch, scale, and key.
- The student will recognize and apply key signatures.

(2) Learn and use scale systems, key relationships, and chord progressions
- The student will describe the triad and the tonic chord.
- The student will sing and recognize whole and half steps in major scales.
- The student will describe and recognize intervals, chords, and triads.
- The student will describe the concepts of measure, barline, and meter.

(3) Recognize musical forms
- The singer will recognize and discuss musical forms, including: ABA, strophic, variation and coda.
- The student will recognize and perform a musical example of canonic form.
- The student will recognize form through repetition and contrast of musical material.

E. Students sight-read, accurately and expressively, music with a level of difficulty of 2 on a scale of 1-6.
(Applies to performing classes only)

(1) Sing and recognize intervals
- The student will recognize and perform melodic and harmonic intervals.
- The student will sight-read exercises which emphasize the tonic chord.
- The student will recognize and perform harmonic intervals in an ensemble.
- The student will practice singing melodic intervals in a short a cappella song.
- The student will describe and recognize intervals, chords, and triads.

(2) Read and sing melodic patterns and harmonic structures in a variety of keys and tonalities, using specific methodology such as solfege or numbers
- The student will sight-read short unison a cappella pieces.
- The student will sight-read short accompanied unison pieces.
- The student will sight-read short accompanied two-, three-, and four-part songs in the keys of C, F, and G major.
- The student will sight-read short a cappella two-, three-, and four-part songs in the keys of C, F, and G major.

6. LISTENING TO, ANALYZING, AND DESCRIBING MUSIC

A. Students describe specific musical events in a given aural example, using appropriate terminology.

(1) The student will listen to a recording and describe the musical events in a specified choral work using the terminology with which he/she is presently working (e.g., describe the polyphonic entrances of soprano, alto, tenor and bass; aurally discriminate between examples of monophony, homophony and polyphony).

(2) The student will use appropriate terminology to describe recordings of his/her own performances.

B. Students analyze the uses of elements of music in aural examples representing diverse genres and cultures.

(1) The student will compare and contrast diverse types of choral music techniques (e.g. jazz tone quality vs. Renaissance tone quality, or dynamic contrasts in spirituals vs. that of the Baroque).

(2) The student will compare and contrast tone quality among diverse musical types such as traditional choral music, gospel music, country-western groups, ensemble music of China, and that of the Middle East.

(3) The student will discuss and analyze the musical characteristics of a madrigal, spiritual, or American folk song.

C. Students demonstrate knowledge of the basic principles of meter, rhythm, tonality, intervals, chords, and harmonic progressions in their analyses of music.

(1) The student will discuss musical elements, including meter and rhythm, present in a recording of choral music.

(2) The student will discuss musical elements, including tonality, melodic and harmonic intervals, and harmonic progressions of I, IV, and V.

7. EVALUATING MUSIC AND MUSIC PERFORMANCES

A. Students develop criteria for evaluating the quality and effectiveness of music performances and compositions and apply the criteria in their personal listening and performing.

(1) Critical Evaluation: Monitoring progress toward musical goals
  • The student will monitor progress toward musical goals by noting development of his/her individual range.
  • The student will monitor progress toward a musical goal by listening to early and more recent rehearsal recordings to note improvement in such choral techniques as intonation, vowel shapes, balance, and blend of the ensemble.

(2) Critical Evaluation: Evaluate self both as a solo and ensemble performer
  • The student will listen critically to self and the chorus, concentrating on the balance and blend of the voice parts.

(3) Critical Evaluation: Evaluate self and others' solo and group rehearsals and/or performances
  • The student will evaluate self as a solo performer by taping himself/herself singing at the end of the year as compared with the beginning of the year.
  • The student will evaluate progress as an ensemble performer by listening critically to tapes, comparing polished performances with early rehearsals of a specific work.

(4) Citizenship Through Group Endeavor: Working effectively as a responsible team member
  • The student will work effectively with others as a responsible team member by performing in small ensembles, creating original choreography in groups, and supporting efforts of the group through suggestions, encouragement, and enthusiasm.

(5) Citizenship Through Group Endeavor: Developing leadership abilities
- The student will develop leadership abilities by serving as student director, designing and teaching original choreography, leading a small ensemble, and acting as a section leader during rehearsal and/or sight-reading sessions.

B. Students evaluate the quality and effectiveness of their own and others' performances, compositions, arrangements, and improvisations by applying specific criteria appropriate for the style of the music and offer constructive suggestions for improvement.

(1) Evaluate own and others' solo and group rehearsals and/or performances
- The student will evaluate his own and other's solo and group rehearsals and/or performances.
- The student will listen critically to self and the chorus, concentrating on the balance and blend of the voice parts.
- The student will listen critically to self and the chorus, concentrating on such choral techniques as intonation, diction, memorization, uniform vowels, and choral tone quality.
- The student will evaluate progress as an ensemble performer by listening critically to tapes comparing polished performances with early rehearsals of a specific work.

8. UNDERSTANDING RELATIONSHIPS BETWEEN MUSIC, THE OTHER ARTS, AND DISCIPLINES OUTSIDE THE ARTS

A. Students compare, in two or more arts, how the characteristic materials of each art can be used to transform similar events, scenes, emotions, or ideas into works of art.

(1) The student will translate monophonic movement in music into monophonic movement in visual art or dance.

(2) The student will combine history, drama, and music for an in-class presentation.

(3) The student will combine the art forms of drama and music.

(4) The student will combine drama, poetry, dance, and music to create a Shakespearean scene.

B. Students describe ways in which the principles and subject matter of other disciplines taught in the school are interrelated with those of music.

(1) The student will relate a song based on the poetry of [Christina Rossetti] to language arts.

(2) The student will apply language arts skills during music classes by listing different words which mean [pitch].

(3) The student will apply information learned in music [anatomy of the breathing mechanism] to science classes.

(4) The student will describe poetic imagery in a song.

(5) The student will relate information about the ears, nose, and throat to issues of voice production and vocal health.

(6) The student will relate music performed in class with events in American and world history.

9. UNDERSTANDING MUSIC IN RELATION TO HISTORY AND CULTURE

A. Students describe distinguishing characteristics of representative music genres and styles from a variety of cultures.

(1) Hearing, identifying, describing, and performing music from a variety of musical styles, eras, and composers.
- The student will develop an understanding of the Western choral tradition, American spirituals, international folk songs, American jazz style, and the choral music of various countries through discussion, listening, and performance.
- The student will learn to sing in a variety of styles, (i.e. legato, jazz swing, Renaissance tone quality vs. Romantic tone quality, etc.).

(2) Recognizing similarities and differences between choral styles of the major historical periods
- The student will recognize and describe similarities and differences among choral styles of the past and present.
- The student will perform literature and discuss characteristics of the Renaissance, Baroque, Classical, Romantic, and Twentieth Century eras.

B. Students classify by genre, style, historical period, composer, and title a varied body of exemplary musical works and explain the characteristics that cause each work to be considered exemplary.

(1) Recognizing similarities and differences between choral styles of the major historical periods
- The student will recognize and describe similarities and differences among choral styles of the past and present.
- The student will perform literature and discuss characteristics of the Renaissance, Baroque, Classical, Romantic, and Twentieth Century eras.
- The student will perform dynamic and tempo changes as indicated by the composer.
- The student will identify geographic regions and discuss the music from those regions.
- The student will compare and contrast music today with music of 400 years ago.
- The student will research music sung by persons of his/her grandparents' generation.
- The student will write an essay comparing popular songs of today with those of the Renaissance.

C. Students compare, in several cultures of the world, functions music serves, roles of musicians, and conditions under which music is typically performed.

(1) The student will explore careers in the field of music.

(2) The student will research (through books, video, and other media) the role of musicians around the world.

(3) The student will study how music is used in various cultures by researching, discussing, and, where appropriate, demonstrating a specified time or place (colonial America, African folk song, etc.).

CANTATE DOMINO (SING TO THE LORD, OUR GOD)

Composer: Giuseppi Ottavio Pitoni (1657-1743), edited by John Reed

Text: Latin, from the Biblical Psalms, English translation by James Pruett

Ranges:

Voicing: SATB a cappella
Key: G minor
Meter: 3/4 (in one)
Form: Through-composed
Style: Motet

Accompaniment: a cappella
Programming: Concert, Contest, or Festival

Ranges:

Soprano · Alto · Tenor · Bass

Student Book Page 1

CANTATE DOMINO (SING TO THE LORD, OUR GOD)

Composer: Giuseppi Ottavio Pitoni (1657-1743), edited by John Reed
Text: Latin Psalm Text, English Translation by James Pruett
Voicing: SATB a cappella

Cultural Context:
Giuseppi Pitoni (1657-1743) was an eminent church musician who lived in Italy during the *Baroque Period*. Sacred choral music was very important at this time and many church composers continued to write in the polyphonic choral style that was popular a century earlier in the *Renaissance*. Pitoni used all Latin texts in his sacred works like "Cantante Domino." His music often incorporated *polyphony* (each voice is equally important and enters at a different time) with occasional *homophony* (music in which the parts move together with the same rhythm).

During this period, musical notation was still developing; as a result, metrical barlines, dynamics, and other style markings were not included in the music. The markings you see in this edition were all added by the editor, John Reed. Sometimes, the meter shifts for a brief time. Notice how the triple meter changes in measures 25-30.

(m. 25)

Where else does this meter shift occur? This shifting is called *hemiola*.

Musical Terms:

allegro

mf (mezzo forte)

ƥ (fermata)

f (forte)

mp (mezzo piano)

polyphony

homophony

hemiola

cresc. (crescendo)

(decrescendo)

p (piano)

Preparation:
Practice saying the Latin words in the phonetic pronunciation guide below.

Cantate Domino, canticum novum:
KAHN-tah-teh DAW-mee-naw KAHN-tee-koom NAW-voom

Laus ejus in Ecclesia Sanctorum,
LAH(oo)s EH-yoos een eh-KLEH-zee-ah SAHNK-taw-řoom

Laetetur Israel in eo,
leh-TEH-tooř EEZ-řah-ehl een EH-aw

Qui fecit eum: et filiae Sion, exultent in rege suo.
quee FEH-cheet EH-oom eht FEE-lee-eh SEE-awn ehk-ZOOL-tehnt een ŘEH-jeh SOO-aw

*ř = flipped or rolled r.

Practice your good choral skills by repeating the following words with good, tall, open vowel sounds.

Evaluation:
Speak the text in rhythm in the following ways and evaluate your Latin pronunciation and rhythmic precision.

- All together
- In sections

1

Objectives:

- The student will develop proper Latin diction through the correct use of vowel shapes and syllabic stress. (*National Standard* 1A)
- The student will perform literature and discuss characteristics of the early Baroque period. (*NS* 6B, 9A)

Historical/Stylistic Guidelines:

In eighteenth century choral music, sacred works were greatly influenced by the secular compositions of the day, particularly opera. Giuseppi Pitoni (1657-1743) was one of the few composers to retain the earlier style and tradition of Giovanni Palestrina. Like Palestrina, Pitoni was a prolific writer of the Roman school. Pitoni copied Palestrina's style of writing sacred works that were based on secular madrigals. He also imitated Palestrina's style of consonance, dissonance, counterpoint, and vocal polyphony.

By the time Pitoni was five years old he was known as an outstanding student and chorister. At age sixteen, he was named maestro di cappella (director of church music) at Terra di Rotundo. He also held similar jobs at Assisi, St. Peters, and San Marco, where he is buried. While at St. Peters he composed complete church services for the entire year. Pitoni spent a great deal of time rescoring many of Palestrina's works. He also completed a history of the Roman musicians.

Music from this time period is extremely effective for younger choirs. The young female voice is an excellent substitution for the male soprano and male alto voices that were used centuries ago. During this time in history, women were not allowed to be a part of the church service. Also, most of the choirs had no more than twenty-four singers.

Many important historical events occurred during Pitoni's lifetime. Such events include the construction of Buckingham Palace in London and Isaac Newton's formulation of the law of gravity. Other important musicians of the day include Henry Purcell, Heinrich Schütz, Dietrich Buxtehude, Johann Sebastian Bach, Domenico Scarlatti, and George Frideric Handel.

Vocal Technique/Warm-Ups/Exercises:

Rehearse each cadence many times to be sure that it is in tune before proceeding to the next section. Practice the cadences written below. Be sure that the raised third at each cadence is in tune. Practice the same type of drill at measures 15, 39, and 43. Sing on a neutral syllable "too."

Rehearsal Guidelines And Notes
Suggested Sequence:

1. Familiarize students with the musical terms found in this piece as listed in the student text. (*NS 5C*)
2. Discuss the material found in the Cultural Context on the student page.
3. Learn the pitches to the opening phrase (mm. 1-6). Be sure that the stress is on beat one and the eighth note runs are clean and clear. For clarity, rehearse the runs on the syllable "ta."
4. Discuss the material on hemiola found on the student page before introducing the middle section ("Lae-te-tur" at m. 20). Keep the quarter note constant throughout this section.
5. Isolate the "ex-ul-tant" section at m. 33. Rehearse the bass and soprano together and the tenor and alto parts together. Some time should be spent explaining to the singers how they find their pitches throughout this section.
6. Next, add the Latin one phrase at a time. (See the Preparation section of the student page for the pronunciation guide.)
7. Sing through "Cantate Domino" in its entirety. Identify any sections that need re-teaching.
8. Be sure that the students pay particular attention to the dynamics indicated in the score by the editor.

Performance Tips:

- In "Cantate Domino," Pitoni avoids sameness by exploring rhythmic changes, a device commonly used by Palestrina. These changes, found in measure 38, include accented syllables falling on any of the beats (weak or strong). The listener hears the combination of triple, duple, and single beat rhythms. These hemiolas can be found in the middle section of "Cantate Domino."
- This piece should be felt in one (one beat per measure).
- Insist that the singers stress beat one more strongly than beats two and three.
- The tone should be light and free with lots of rhythmic vitality and energy.
- The eighth notes in measure 12 should be treated as pick-up notes and should be unaccented and "lean into" measure 13.
- All long phrases should be sung with staggered breathing.
- If tuning and/or ranges are a problem, begin "Cantate Domino" up or down a half step.

Evaluation:

Speak the rhythm to "Cantate Domino" in the following ways: (*NS 7A, 7B*)

- All together
- In sections

Listen carefully to a tape of the choir singing "Cantate Domino," check for the following: (*NS 7A, 7B*)

- Light tone, not too heavy
- Cadences in tune
- Long sustained phrases with staggered breathing

Extension:

Play a recording of other works from this time period.

Cantate Domino

(Sing To The Lord, Our God)

For SATB a cappella

English translation by JAMES PRUETT

By GIUSEPPI OTTAVIO PITONI (1657-1743)
Edited and Arranged by JOHN REED

Student Book Page 2

4

Student
Book Page
3

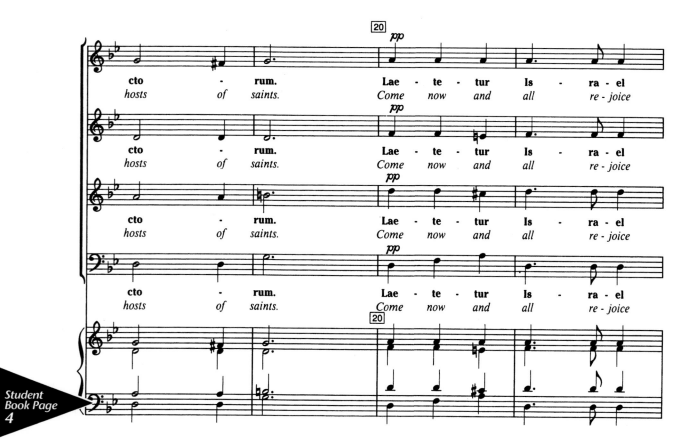

6

7

8

Student
Book Page
7

9

DIDN'T MY LORD DELIVER DANIEL

Composer: Traditional Spiritual, arranged by Roger Emerson
Text: Traditional
Voicing: 3-Part Mixed

Key: F minor
Meter: 4/4
Form: Strophic with imitation
Style: Syncopated spiritual
Accompaniment: Piano

Programming: Good early-in-the-year piece; limited ranges; much unison and repetition; immediate success; features driving rhythm in a pop style idiom.

Ranges:

DIDN'T MY LORD DELIVER DANIEL

Composer: Spiritual adapted and arranged by Roger Emerson
Text: Traditional
Voicing: 3-Part Mixed

Student Book Page 8

Cultural Context:

Spirituals developed in America before the Civil War when slaves turned to Biblical stories to create music of hope and relief from oppression and suffering. In this spiritual, if the Lord could deliver Daniel from a den of lions and Jonah from the belly of a whale, why could the Lord not deliver the slaves from bondage?

Musical Terms:

(♩ = 80)   (♩ = 132-144)   *mp* (mezzo piano)

mf (mezzo forte)   *cresc.* (crescendo)   *f* (forte)

unis. (unison)   div. (divisi)   ⊤ (tenuto)

rit. (ritardando)   ≥ (accent)   ⊕ Coda

D.S. al Coda   𝄋 (sign)   **To Coda**

⌢ (fermata)   syncopation

Preparation:

Syncopation is a rhythmic pattern that stresses notes on the "offbeat." Practice these syncopated patterns:

Notice how much rhythmic energy syncopation adds. Syncopated rhythm is a characteristic of African-American spirituals and now is used in many other styles of music.

Evaluation:
• Record the choir singing this song. When you listen, quietly tap or conduct the steady beat. Do you hear and feel the syncopation in this song?

• What other spirituals of deliverance or hope have you sung or heard? Share your experiences in small or large group discussion.

Objectives:

- The student will perform syncopated rhythms with understanding and accuracy. *(National Standard 1E)*
- The student will develop an understanding of the American Spiritual through discussion and performance. *(NS 6B, 9A)*

Historical/Stylistic Guidelines:

Discuss the material found in Cultural Context on the student page. Other familiar spirituals include "Sinner Man," (p. 141), "Swing Low, Sweet Chariot," "Deep River," "I'm Gonna Sing," "I Wanna Be Ready," "Every Time I Feel the Spirit," "Ezekiel Saw the Wheel," "Mary and Martha," "Peter, Go Ring Dem Bells," and "I Got Shoes."

Vocal Technique/Warm-Ups/Exercises:

Articulation is the action of the lips, teeth, and tip of the tongue in making sounds. Strong consonants help maintain the energy required for syncopated singing. Encourage students to exaggerate the movement of their mouths (over articulate) while singing the following exercise to practice strong consonants.

Did - n't   my   Lord __ de - li - ver   Dan - iel ___

Sing in octaves with Part III. Ascend by half steps to C and descend by half steps back to A.

Rehearsal Guidelines And Notes
Suggested Sequence:

1. Familiarize students with the musical terms found in this piece as listed in the student text. *(NS 5C)*
2. Begin with the unison A sections (mm. 5-13, 16-24, and 33-40). First, have the students chant the words in rhythm, checking for accuracy and crisp articulation. Add the pitches.
3. Now focus attention on the B sections of the song (mm. 25-32 and 50-57). How do they differ from the A sections? (Three part harmony, different rhythms and text, homophony) Have students chant the words in rhythm together. Teach or have students read and sing their individual parts. Sing together.
4. Students are now prepared to sing mm. 1-40. Re-teach any problem areas.
5. Focus on mm. 41-48. Ask students if this is like any other section they have learned. (It is different.) Again, have students chant words in rhythm checking for accuracy and crisp articulation. Teach or have students read and sing their individual parts. Sing together.
6. Teach the coda. Return to the beginning and sing the entire song. Check constantly for rhythmic accuracy and strong consonants with emphasis on the syncopation.
7. Sing the song again using dynamic markings as indicated in the score.

Performance Tips:

- Emphasize the consonants to energize the tone.
- Make a contrast in style between the slower legato opening and the faster, driving rock style that follows in m.12.
- If the singers are having difficulty perfecting the syncopated style of this piece, have them snap on beats 2 and 4 of each measure.
- To increase precision and energy, have students whisper texts in rhythm exaggerating the consonants.

Evaluation:

Follow the Evaluation as it appears on the student page:

- Record the choir singing this song. When you listen, quietly tap or conduct the steady beat. Do you hear and feel the syncopation in this song?
- What other spirituals of deliverance have you sung or heard? Discuss these other songs.

Extension:

- Listen to recordings of famous spirituals. Discuss what the students hear on the recordings. Based on the discussions, ask students to identify what they could do to improve their own performance of "Didn't My Lord Deliver Daniel."
- Encourage students to prepare a solo performance of a spiritual for class or concert.

Suggested Recordings:

"I'm Goin' to Sing." The Robert Shaw Chorale, Robert Shaw, conductor. LSC 2580.
"Swing Low, Sweet Chariot." Leontyne Price, soprano. RCA LSC-2600.

Didn't My Lord Deliver Daniel

For 3-Part Mixed Voices and Piano

Traditional Spiritual
Adapted and Arranged by ROGER EMERSON

Student Book Page 11

17

DING DONG! MERRILY ON HIGH!

Composer: Traditional Carols, Arranged by Ed Lojeski
Text: Traditional
Voicing: SATB a cappella
Key: G Major

Meter: Cut-time
Form: Through-composed
Style: Contemporary
Accompaniment: a cappella

Programming: Holiday concert, caroling, easy to learn; students will feel successful; small ensemble

Ranges:

Student Book Page **16**

DING DONG! MERRILY ON HIGH!

Composer: Traditional carols, arranged by Ed Lojeski
Text: Traditional
Voicing: SATB a cappella

Cultural Context:
This arrangement is a lively setting of the 16th century French carol "Ding Dong! Merrily on High!," combined with the 16th century English carol "Good King Wenceslas." In addition, the arranger has added a *madrigal*-like contrasting section which introduces and then accompanies "Good King Wenceslas."

Musical Terms:

f (forte) p (piano) pp (pianissimo)

ff (fortissimo)   *cresc.* (crescendo)   (fermata)

Preparation:
Practice singing the passage below:

1. Practice it once using the syllable "too." Be sure to stress the first beat of every measure.

2. Practice singing it again on the text, using the following dynamics:
   - 1st time – forte
   - 2nd time – pianissimo

Practice saying the words written below using the word stress indicated.

HIGH - est   SING - ing   GLO - ry   RING - ing

Evaluation:
Record your choir singing "Ding Dong! Merrily on High!" Listen for the following:

1. Word Stress – Are you stressing the first syllable more than the second of the words listed above?

2. Dynamic change – Are you singing the dynamics marked in the score?

3. Rhythmic precision – On the long "Gloria" phrases, can you hear the separate notes clearly?

Objectives:

- The student will sing with energy and clear diction. (*National Standard* 1A)
- The student will learn to sing with correct syllable stress. (*NS* 1E)
- The student will perform seasonal choral literature. (*NS* 1E)

Historical/Stylistic Guidelines:

This arrangement combines the French carol "Ding Dong! Merrily on High!" with the English carol "Good King Wenceslas." In Medieval times a carol was originally known as a round dance with musical accompaniment. Today a carol is widely known as a song for the celebration of Christmas. "Ding Dong! Merrily on High!" is among the most famous of the French carols. French carols are called noëls. "Good King Wenceslas" is a very famous English carol that dates back to 1582 where it was listed in the *Pia Cantonus*, a Medieval collection of songs. In its original form, "Good King Wenceslas" was a spring carol and did not appear in its present Christmas form until 1853.

Vocal Technique/Warm-Ups/Exercises:

1. Articulation is the action of the lips, teeth, and tip of the tongue in making sounds. (Remind the students that singing is exaggerated speech.)

   Practice the following exercise to enforce the importance of good articulation.

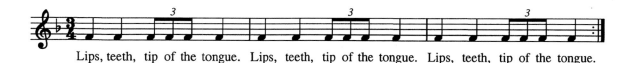

Lips, teeth, tip of the tongue. Lips, teeth, tip of the tongue. Lips, teeth, tip of the tongue.

   Repeat exercise up by half steps.

2. Discuss the following forms of articulation:

   a. staccato - detached, very short. Shorten the notes by 1/2.
   b. legato - bound together, very smooth and connected.
   c. semi-staccato - a combination of the above, shorten the notes by 1/4.

After the notes are secure, ask the students to sing mm. 9-24 and mm. 25-48 using the forms of articulation listed above. The semi-staccato style will probably work the best. If the singers can hear the difference in styles of articulation, then they will be able to produce the proper style for this piece. This can make an excellent warm-up after the piece has been introduced.

Rehearsal Guidelines And Notes
Suggested Sequence:

1. Familiarize students with the musical terms found in this piece as listed in the student text. (*NS 5C*)

2. The pitches are not terribly difficult, so this selection will work well as a tool to sharpen sightreading skills.

3. As you begin singing on the words, review with the singers the material on word stress found on the student page.

4. Rehearse mm.1-25 as section A, and mm. 25-66 as section B, and mm. 66-91 as section C. This piece breaks up very well into individual units.

5. When you begin work on section B, discuss the three forms of articulation discussed in part 2 of Vocal Technique listed above.

6. At measure 57, the high D entrance in the bass part on the word "brightly" can cause tuning difficulties. Practice it in the following ways:

   a. Practice the yawn sigh down from a high D down the octave to the D in the music.

   b. Repeat the exercise on the "ah" vowel.

   c. Sing the line as written.

7. At m. 66, the tenor part may be too low for some of the singers. Have them drop out until m. 76. (The basses are singing the same part.)

8. Isolate the last line (mm. 88-91) and teach it separately. The melodic pattern and rhythmic pattern change drastically here.

9. Sing "Ding Dong! Merrily on High!" in its entirety. Identify any sections that need re-teaching.

10. Make sure that the choir is making the most of the dynamic changes listed in the music.

Performance Tips:

- "Ding Dong! Merrily on High!" should be sung with a light, "madrigal-like" approach. Each vocal part should sound like one voice.

- The "fa-la-la" sections should be very crisp and clean since they are nonsense syllables. The other three parts should sing softer at the bass entrance at m. 49.

- If the articulation is still not as clean as you would like, have the students whisper the section. Whispering can correct careless articulation. Remind the singers that the mouth should be open more in singing than in speech.

- Keeping a steady tempo should be a priority when teaching this piece. This piece can rush if a strict pulse is not kept.

- Work for clear, crisp, exaggerated consonants throughout "Ding Dong! Merrily on High!"

- This piece works well for a small group for caroling in the halls or performing in the community.

Evaluation:

Listen for the following as you sing this piece: (*NS 7A, 7B*)

1. Word stress. Are you stressing the first syllable more than the second syllable in the words listed on the student page?

2. Dynamic change. Do you hear the changes marked in the score?

3. Rhythmic precision. In the long "Gloria" phrases, can you hear the separate notes clearly?

Extension:

Play a recording of a school or professional choir singing either of these carols.

Ding Dong! Merrily On High!

For SATB a cappella

Performance Notes: Keep tempo bright throughout. This arrangement can be performed by any size group with a minimum of rehearsal time.

Old French Carol
Arranged by ED LOJESKI (ASCAP)

Student Book Page 17

24

26

Student
Book Page
21

Fa la la la la la la. Fa la la fa la la

Fa la la la. Fa la la

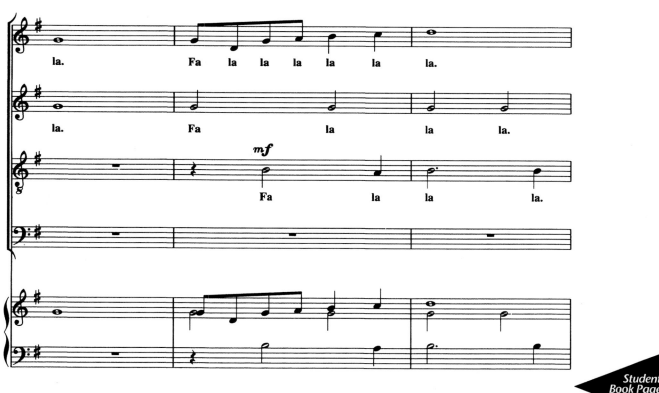

la. Fa la la la la la la.

la. Fa la la la.

_mf_

Fa la la la.

Student Book Page 23

34

ECCE QUAM BONUM (SEE HOW GOOD, HOW RIGHT)

Composer: Jean Richafort (1480-1548), edited by Maynard Klein
Text: Latin text adapted from Psalm 133
Voicing: SATB a cappella

Key: G Major
Meter: 3/4, 4/4
Form: AB
Style: Renaissance polyphonic motet, text emphasizes unity and brotherhood

Accompaniment: a cappella
Programming: Contest, concert, festival; excellent piece to teach Renaissance style

Ranges:

Student
Book Page
32

ECCE QUAM BONUM (SEE HOW GOOD, HOW RIGHT)

Composer: Jean Richafort (1480-1548), edited by Maynard Klein
Text: Latin text adapted from Psalm 133
Voicing: SATB a cappella

Cultural Context:
Jean Richafort (ca. 1480-1548) lived during a time period known as the *Renaissance* (1450-1600). The Renaissance is sometimes called the "Golden Age of A Cappella Music" because of the large number of unaccompanied choral pieces written during that time.

"Ecce Quam Bonum," like other Renaissance choral music, is *polyphonic*. Polyphonic means that each voice is equally important and enters at a different time throughout the piece. Notice the polyphonic entrances in "Ecce Quam Bonum."

Many characteristics of our modern musical notation were developed after this music was written. The meter, barlines, and style words (dynamics, tempo markings, articulations) were all added by the editor, and are only suggestions for how the music should be performed.

Musical Terms:

a cappella	polyphonic	Renaissance
melisma	allegro	($\quad$ = c. 120)
mf (mezzo forte)	*mp* (mezzo piano)	animato
f (forte)	*ff* (fortissimo)	legato
staccato		(crescendo and decrescendo)

Preparation:
Melismas (patterns which contain more than one note per word syllable) may be a challenge in this piece. Use the following exercise to practice singing melismas cleanly. Do not let notes run together.

1. Sing the notes staccato (short) on a neutral syllable.
2. Sing the notes legato (connected).
3. Separate the notes just slightly (a combination of legato and staccato).

Evaluation:
Look at your music and circle the melismas in your part. Your circles should remind you to sing these patterns cleanly without running the notes together. As you rehearse "Ecce Quam Bonum," check to see if you are performing the melismas cleanly.

(Answers to melisma question in student Evaluation)
Soprano: circle mm. 28, 30, 31
Alto: circle mm. 2, 7, 28, 30
Tenor: circle mm. 24, 25, 26, 31
Bass: circle mm. 4, 9, 25, 30

Objectives:

- The student will develop breath control adequate for performing melismas. (*National Standard* 1A)
- The student will develop proper Latin diction through the use of correct vowel shapes and syllabic stress. (*NS* 1C)

Historical/Stylistic Guidelines:

Jean Richafort was a French-speaking Netherlander who served as choir master for many large churches. He may have been a student of Josquin des Prez and is believed to have written motets for Louis XII of France. He was considered a master of counterpoint, as illustrated by "Ecce Quam Bonum," and followed Josquin in his efforts to enhance the relationship between words and music. His works include motets, chansons, and parody masses.

The *motet,* of which "Ecce Quam Bonum" is an example, is considered to be the most important form of polyphonic music during Medieval and Renaissance periods. Although its definition varied widely, a motet from the Renaissance Period is usually an unaccompanied choral composition based on a Latin sacred text.

Psalm 133 (King James Version) reads: "Behold, how good and how pleasant it is for brethren to dwell together in unity!" Note the English lyrics printed in the music are sacred, but the Latin text, as quoted directly from the Bible, is not directly religious in content.

Vocal Technique/Warm-Ups/Exercises:

To emphasize pure Latin vowels, use the following exercise as a warm-up:
- Sing the exercise with a raised soft palate.
- Emphasize "ah" (not "uh") and "leh" (not "lay").

Use the melisma exercise in the student Preparation section as an additional warm-up.

Rehearsal Guidelines And Notes
Suggested Sequence:

1. Familiarize students with the musical terms found in this piece as listed in the student text. (*NS* 5C)
2. Initially, learn only the 3/4 section.
3. Isolate rhythms from pitch by making an overhead transparency of the following exercise:
   - Chant rhythms with soprano/tenor and alto/bass parts separately.
   - The exercise is based on mm. 1-11 and could be extended to include the entire 3/4 section.

4. Using the score, combine all four parts and rehearse until singers are proficient with the rhythms of the polyphonic entrances.

5. Sight-read the pitches of the 3/4 section. Note that soprano and tenor have very similar pitches, as do altos and basses. Rehearsing soprano and tenor together, or bass and alto together will result in a canon. Note also that the alto-soprano combination is imitated by the bass-tenor. Rehearse each voice in combination (AB, ST, SA, TB) before combining all four parts.

6. Following a similar procedure, learn the rhythms and then the pitches to the 4/4 section. Rehearse until the singers are proficient.

7. Learn the text. Latin is much preferred over English in this piece because the natural word stress falls on the correct beats and it is an opportunity to teach pure, uniform vowels.

Latin: *Ecce quam bonum*
Pronunciation: EH-cheh quahm BAW-noom

et quam jucundum
eht quahm yoo-KOON-doom

habitare, fratres in unum
ah-bee-TAH-r̃eh FR̃AH-tr̃ehs een OO-noom

alleluia.
ah-leh-LOO-yah

r̃ = rolled or flipped r

8. Speak isolated words (singers echo your speaking). Speak words in rhythm using the score. Finally, sing words with pitches using the score.

9. Identify and rehearse the sections that need re-teaching.

10. Remind the students to pay particular attention to the word stress and dynamics suggested by the editor in the score.

Performance Tips:

- Typical Latin problem areas include:

j = y (jucundum)	cc = ch (ecce)	h = silent (habitare)
flip or roll all r's	i = ee (in)	e = eh (habitare & alleluia)

- To teach independence of line and still encourage singers to listen to every section, stand each section in a circle (huddle) so they can hear each other within the section. When secure, open each circle slightly. Later, rehearse in a single large circle, then return to traditional riser formation.

- Record rehearsals frequently to check for vowel uniformity, clarity of parts, and intonation.

- Emphasize initial pitch of each polyphonic entrance. Asking students to sing only their entrance pitch and whisper the rest of the phrase will increase awareness of other voice parts besides their own.

- Balance the imitative sections carefully, reminding singers that no individual voice part should be louder than another.

- Conduct the 3/4 section in 1 to maintain a dance-like feeling.

- Increase the intensity across each held note to add energy to the sound.

- Perform with the suggested tempo changes and dynamic contrasts.

Evaluation:

- Check that singers have circled melismas as mentioned in the student Evaluation section. (*NS 7A, 7B*)

- To evaluate Latin vowels, videotape students singing the "alleluia" exercise in the Vocal Technique section. With singers standing in rows, videotape the front row as all rows sing. Focus the camera on the mouth of each singer and pan down the front row. Move the front row to back and bring the next row up. Continue the process until all rows are taped. This procedure keeps everyone busy, serves as a warm-up, and allows the director to evaluate how each student is shaping his/her vowels. (*NS 7A, 7B*)

Ecce Quam Bonum

(See How Good, How Right)

For SATB a cappella

Psalm 133
Adapted by M. K.

Music by JEAN RICHAFORT (c. 1480-1548)
Edited by MAYNARD KLEIN

43

GLORIA FESTIVA

Composer: Emily Crocker
Text: Traditional Latin with
  additional words by
  Emily Crocker
Voicing: 3-Part Mixed

Key: F Major; A Major; G Major
Meter: 4/4
Form: ABACA' coda
Style: Contemporary, festive, sacred
Accompaniment: Piano

Programming: Concert or festival

Ranges:

GLORIA FESTIVA

Composer: Emily Crocker
Text: Traditional Latin with additional words by Emily Crocker
Voicing: 3-Part Mixed

**Student
Book Page
36**

Cultural Context:

"Gloria Festiva" was written in 1993 by Emily Crocker, a Texas native who now lives and composes in Milwaukee, Wisconsin. She has published music since 1980, and has over 100 choral pieces in print. A portion of the text in "Gloria Festiva" is traditional Latin.

Musical Terms:

(♩ = ca. 132)	*mp* (mezzo piano)	*mf* (mezzo forte)
ff (fortissimo)	*decresc.* (decrescendo)	⌢ (fermata)
cresc. (crescendo)	*dolce*	*al fine*
maestoso	*rit.* (ritardando)	opt. div. (optional divisi)
descant	*f* (forte)	(no breath)

Preparation:

Pronunciation: *Gloria in excelsis Deo,*
  GLAW-řee-ah een ehk-SHEHL-sees DEH-aw

  et in terra pax hominibus.
  eht een TEH-řah pahks aw-MEE-nee-boos

  *ř = flipped or rolled r.

Translation: Glory to God in the highest, and peace on earth to all.

• Tap, clap, or count the rhythm pattern below. Be sure to observe the rest on the second half of beat 3 in the first measure of the phrase.

• Chant the Latin words to this rhythm.

  Glo-ri - a _____ in ex-cel-sis De - o et in ter-ra pax ho-mi - ni-bus

Evaluation:

To perform this song successfully, sing pure Latin vowels with rhythmic accuracy. As you sing the first 22 measures, answer the following questions:

1. Did I sing with tall, pure Latin vowels?
2. Did my vowel sounds blend with the other singers around me?
3. Did I sing the words in precise rhythm?
4. Was I rhythmically precise with the other singers around me?
5. Did I sing with energy?

As you master the song, continue to evaluate your progress.

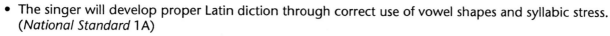

Objectives:

- The singer will develop proper Latin diction through correct use of vowel shapes and syllabic stress. (*National Standard* 1A)
- The singer will listen critically to self as an individual and as a participating member of an ensemble. (*NS* 7A, 7B)

Historical/Stylistic Guidelines:

"Gloria Festiva" is a festive, energetic work. It is written with contrast in rhythmic drive and dynamic levels between the opening A section and the middle B and C sections. This is not to say that the softer B and C sections are sung without energy. "Gloria Festiva" may serve as an excellent program opener or closer. Your students should have great fun with it!

Emily Crocker lives and works in Milwaukee, Wisconsin. She taught public school music in Texas for fifteen years before joining the music publishing industry.

Vocal Technique/Warm-Ups/Exercises:

- Review the material found in the Preparation section on the student page to practice the rhythms and Latin pronunciation used in this song.
- Practice the following exercise to help develop the breath support needed for the long, sustained phrases at m. 41.

Rehearsal Guideline And Notes
Suggested Sequence:

1. Familiarize students with the musical terms found in this piece as listed in the student text. (*NS* 5C)
2. Practice the Latin pronunciation as described in the Cultural Context section on the student page.
3. All students chant the words in rhythm mm. 5-13; check for Latin pronunciation and rhythmic accuracy. Since this motive is sung several times throughout the piece, ask all singers (not just Part III) to rehearse the opening in an appropriate octave.
4. Teach mm. 13-21 isolating the measures that are sung in parts.
5. Skip over to m. 31. It is very similar to the material just learned. Teach mm. 31-39.
6. Skip to mm. 59-67. Ask Part III to sing the familiar melody. Teach Parts I and II the harmony. (Save the descant for later.) Combine the three parts. Then teach mm. 68-end where the tempo broadens to a powerful finish.
7. Return to mm. 41-58. Teach this contrasting legato section by emphasizing the long sustained phrases. It is important that Part I and II sing in 4-bar phrases with no break or breath after the words "rejoice," "fear," "love," and "peace." For example: (mm. 41-44) "Come all rejoice in the light."
8. Introduce mm. 23-30 as smooth and legato, with a contrast in rhythmic drive from the opening section. Develop a rise and fall of each phrase. Measure 30 should crescendo into measure 31.
9. Finally, teach the descant.
10. Rehearse the entire song remembering: tall, pure vowels; correct syllabic stress; rhythmic accuracy; contrast in style; and observing all dynamic markings indicated in the score.

Performance Tips:

- To assist in singing 4-bar phrases at m. 41, ask Parts I and II to draw a large rainbow arch in the air with one arm as they sing.

- It may be necessary to practice the entrance at m. 41 several times. Parts I and II may experience some difficulty in singing securely in the new key. The same is true for the key change at m. 49.

- The undesired stressing of unstressed syllables is a common problem for singers. Check for syllabic stress accuracy in the following Latin words: "GLAW-ree-ah," not "glaw-ree-AH"; "DEH-aw" not "deh-AW." Latin utilizes tall, pure vowels.

Evaluation:

- Review the process of evaluation as described in the Evaluation section on the student page. Allow students time to discuss or write down their answers. (*NS 7A, 7B*)

- To evaluate individual Latin diction, as well as accuracy of rhythm and pitches, place a small hand-held recorder or microphone at the end of a row in your choir. As the chorus performs "Gloria Festiva," ask each singer to sing into the microphone for approximately thirty seconds. Ask the singer to pass the recorder to the person standing next to him or her. Repeat this process until everyone in that row has individually sung into the recorder or microphone. The chorus may have to sing the song several times. On another day, record a different row. In the privacy of your office, review and evaluate these tapes. Determine where re-teaching, if any, is necessary. A grade may be given for individual performance. (*NS 7A, 7B*)

Gloria Festiva

For 3-Part Mixed Voices and Piano

Traditional Latin
With additional Words and Music by
EMILY CROCKER (ASCAP)

Glo - ri - a _____ in ex - cel - sis De - o,

et in ter - ra pax ho - mi - ni -

13 Unis.

f

Glo - ri - a _____ in ex - cel - sis De - o,

bus.

et in ter - ra pax ho - mi - ni - bus

Glo - ri - a _____ in ex - cel - sis De - o,

Glo - ri - a _____ in ex - cel - sis De - o,

et in ter - ra pax ho - mi - ni - bus.

et in ter - ra pax ho - mi - ni - bus.

Student
Book Page
39

49

Student
Book Page
43

and grant us peace e - ter - nal, _____

Unis.

____ e - ter - nal _____

e - ter - nal _____

59

Glo - ri - a _____ in ex - cel - sis De - o,

Glo - ri - a _____ in ex - cel - sis De - o, et in ter - ra

Unis.

Glo - ri - a _____ Glo - ri - a _____

pax ho - mi - ni - bus. Glo - ri - a _____ in ex -

Opt. Descant

rit.

Et in ter - ra pax ho -

rit.

_____ in ex - cel - sis. Et in ter - ra pax ho -

rit.

cel - sis De - o Et in ter - ra pax ho -

rit.

Student
Book Page
45

GOOD TIMBER GROWS

Composer: Roger Emerson
Text: Anonymous
Voicing: SATB a cappella

Key: Suggestive of G Minor
Meter: 4/4, 3/4 freely
Form: Through-composed
Style: Contemporary reflective
with expression
Accompaniment: a cappella

Programming: Concert or festival;
thematic program on poetry or
nature; excellent piece to
demonstrate blend, balance, and
tone.

Ranges:

Student Book Page 47

GOOD TIMBER GROWS

Composer: Roger Emerson
Text: Anonymous
Voicing: SATB a cappella

Cultural Context:
Roger Emerson said this about the music he wrote:
"The text is paramount in this selection. Therefore, do not rush, enunciate very clearly, and allow time and space for the textual ideal to become firmly implanted in the listener's mind."

Musical Terms:

(♩ = ca. 69)	adagio	rubato
p (piano)	◠ (fermata)	***mp*** (mezzo piano)
rit. (ritardando)	// (caesura)	*decresc.* (decrescendo)
sub. (subito)	*a tempo*	***f*** (forte)
cresc. poco a poco (crescendo poco a poco)		

Preparation:
Say the words in the text printed below as marked with stressed and unstressed syllables, crescendo and decrescendo. Place your two hands in front of you. Physically move them apart on the crescendo and back together on the decrescendo as if playing an accordian or stretching a rubber band.

p

Good TIM-ber_____DOES not GROW in ease.

mp

Good TIM-ber_____DOES not GROW in ease.

cresc. poco a poco

The STRONG-er WIND, _____the STRONG-er TREES; _____

*sub. **mp***

The FAR-ther sky, _____the GREAT-er length _____

increased intensity

The more the STORMS, the MORE the STRE _____ngth;

mp

By SUN or COLD, _____by RAIN and SNOW, _____

_____ *slowly* _____ *(fade out)*

In TREE or MAN, _____Good TIM-ber GROWS.

Evaluation:
Study the poem (text) carefully. Write a short essay on what the poem means to you. What is the connection between "good people" and "good timber"? Can you find other poetry that compares humankind to nature? Do you enjoy singing this song? Why or why not?

Objectives:

- The singer will develop breath control adequate for supporting sustained phrases. (*National Standard* 1E)
- The student will express sensitivity to the text. (*NS* 1A)
- The singer will perform a piece of music utilizing the musical terminology indicated in the music to interpret the piece as suggested by the composer. (*NS* 5C)

Historical/Stylistic Guidelines:

- Roger Emerson wrote this about "Good Timber Grows":

  The text is paramount in this selection. Therefore, do not rush, enunciate very clearly, and allow time and space for the textual ideal to become firmly implanted in the listener's mind. The length of each fermata and grand pause is arbitrary. However, they should be treated in such a way as to maximize the effect of the text. The entire piece should be performed in a legato, smooth and connected style. For adjudication purposes, unisons, 4ths, 5ths, and triads have been carefully chosen to highlight the ensemble's blend, balance and intonation. The decrescendo on the final chord should end on almost a whisper. I like to use the term "evaporate" to convey the effect, and students should be encouraged to stagger their breathing in order to maintain pitch and vitality.

Vocal Technique/Warm-Ups/Exercises:

To teach long sustained phrases with crescendos and decrescendos, practice the following:

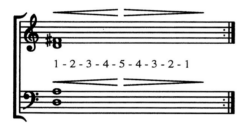

Sing this chord starting very softly then crescendo and decrescendo back to soft. Move the pitch up by half steps when repeated.

Rehearsal Guidelines and Notes
Suggested Sequence:

1. Familiarize students with the musical terms found in this piece as listed in the student text. They are very important to the teaching and performing of this piece. (*NS* 5C)
2. This is an ideal piece for students to sharpen their sightreading skills. Using solfege or numbers, ask students to read their own part. Have them determine if their part moves up or down in a step wise or skipping motion.
3. Sing the parts independently as a sightreading exercise, then on a neutral syllable such as "loo." Sing combined parts on a "loo."

4. Make an overhead transparency or handout of the following. Speak the words practicing the indicated stress and dynamics.

p

Good TIM-ber_____DOES not GROW in ease.

mp

Good TIM-ber_____DOES not GROW in ease.

cresc. poco a poco

The STRONG-er WIND, _____the STRONG-er TREES; _____

sub. mp

The FAR-ther sky, _____the GREAT-er length _____

increased intensity

The more the STORMS, the MORE the STRE _____ngth;

mp

By SUN or COLD, _____by RAIN and SNOW, _____

                                        slowly _____ *(fade out)*

In TREE or MAN, _____Good TIM-ber GROWS.

5. Sing the song in parts with the text.
6. Now sing the song using crescendo, decrescendo, and all other markings indicated in the music. Strive for long sustained phrases and beautiful music making.

Performance Tips:

- Stagger the breathing for longer phrases.
- Create a rise and fall in each phrase.
- Refer to the remarks of Roger Emerson. Apply his suggestions to the performance. Sensitivity to the text is the main purpose of this piece.

Evaluation:

Complete the Evaluation section found on the student page. Encourage students to write an essay and answer all discussion questions. (*NS 7A, 7B*)

Extension:

- Ask the language arts teacher on your campus for suggestions of poetry relating to nature and humankind. (*NS 8A*)
- Create a program based on poetry in word and song using student suggestions.

Good Timber Grows

For SATB a cappella

ANONYMOUS

Music by ROGER EMERSON

Student
Book Page
48

Student
Book Page
49

JU ME LEVE UN BEL MAITÍN (IN THE MORNING I AROSE)

Composer: Anonymous, edited by Robert L. Goodale

Text: Anonymous, 15th Century

Voicing: SATB a cappella

Key: Modal (F Dorian, F Minor)

Meter: 3/4

Form: ABA

Style: Homophonic

Accompaniment: a cappella

Programming: Concert or contest; Very imitative

Ranges:

JU ME LEVE UN BEL MAITÍN (IN THE MORNING I AROSE)

Composer: Anonymous, edited by Robert L. Goodale

Text: Anonymous, 15th Century

Voicing: SATB a cappella

Student Book Page **51**

Cultural Context:

As you read the translation of the text, you will discover that it tells a story. Perhaps the character in the poem lived in the northeast corner of Spain near the French border – thus the use of the three languages: Spanish, French, and Catalan. (Catalan is spoken in the northeast corner of Spain.)

A song of this type is called a *villancico*, a short 16th century song with several stanzas linked by a refrain. The villancico composer often worked with the poet to tell the story with a new style of musical expression.

"Din-di-rin-daña" are nonsense syllables, such as "la-la-la" used today.

The markings (dynamics, tempo, style words) were all added by the editor, Robert L. Goodale.

Musical Terms:

ritard. (ritardando) f (forte)   *poco ritard.* (poco ritardando)

mf (mezzo forte)   (fermata)   *p* (piano)

vivace e leggiero   *pp* (pianissimo)   ¢ (cut time)

‾‾‾‾‾‾‾‾ (crescendo)

Preparation:

Sing the following rhythms on a neutral syllables. Be sure to stress beat 1 more than beats 2 and 3. Practice forte the first time and piano the second time. This exercise should have a light, dance-like quality.

Evaluation:

Record your choir singing this piece and listen for the following:

• Are you stressing beat 1 more than beats 2 and 3?

• Are you singing the dynamics indicated by the editor?

Objectives:

- The student will develop performance techniques that include textual clarity (word accent, syllable stress). (*National Standard* 1E)
- The student will recognize similarities and differences between choral styles of the major historical periods. (*NS* 6B, 9A)

Historical/Stylistic Guidelines:

Review the material found in the Cultural Context section on the student page.

"Ju Me Leve un Bel Maitín" is a villancico. A villancico is defined as "a 15th or 16th century type of Spanish poetry, idyllic or amorous in subject matter consisting of several stanzas linked by a refrain." The refrain in "Ju Me Leve un Bel Maitín" is the "Din di rin" sections of nonsense syllables.

"Ju Me Leve un Bel Maitín" is a typical villancico and should be sung in a light and dance-like style with the feeling of one beat per measure rather than three beats per measure. The shifting meters create a dance-like feel.

Vocal Technique/Warm-Ups/Excercises:

"Ju Me Leve un Bel Maitín" must be sung in a madrigal style with a light clear tone. Practice the following exercise to improve tone production. Each time the excercise should be sung crisply and cleanly (semi-staccato).

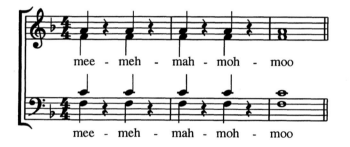

Rehearsal Guidelines And Notes
Suggested Sequence:

1. Familarize students with the musical terms found in this piece as listed in the student text. (*NS 5C*)
2. Practice the pitches in the opening phrase (mm. 1-6) on a neutral syllable "too" or "doo." Point out the two spots where this theme returns (mm. 43-48 and mm. 49-54).
3. Next, learn the pitches at mm. 13-22, again using a neutral syllable. Point out that in mm. 23-32 and mm. 33-42 the pitches are identical to the phrase that they just learned.
4. Introduce the remaining phrase, mm. 7-12. Practice the tenor and soprano together as their parts invert in this phrase.
5 After the pitches are very secure, slowly add the language one phrase at a time. (See the language guide below in the performance tips.)

Performance Tips:

- "Ju Me Leve un Bel Maitín" is not set in a key as we know it today. It is set in a mode.
- This piece should be conducted and performed "in one" (one beat per measure) in the 3/4 measures. Observe the marking (♩. = ♩) when the meter changes. Make sure the overall pulse stays constant. The quarter note does not always stay constant.
- Take extra rehearsal time in helping the sopranos with their high F entrance at m. 7. Practice the yawn-sigh as found on p. 1 of *Essential Musicianship - Book One*.
- Take enough time at the cadences to allow the open 5ths to tune.
- Close to the "n" on the final "Din."
- Place a great deal of stress on the half note "da" in the "din-di-rin" sections.
- The language (or languages) will be your biggest hurdle in teaching this piece. While there are many people that speak Spanish and French, finding someone who is familiar with these dialects and the language of Catalan can be a real challenge.

| French: | *Din-di-rin, din-di-rin, din-di-rin-da-ña, Din-di-rin-din.* |
| Pronunciation: | dihn-dee-rihn dihn-dee-rihn dihn-dee-rihn-DAH-nyah dihn-dee-rihn-dihn |

Ju me leve un bel maitín, Matineta per la prata;
ZHJOO meh LEH-v(eh)oon BEHL mah-TAH MAH-tee-NEH-tah PEHR lah P̃RAH-tah

Encontré le ruyseñor Que cantava so la rama,
AWN-kawn-T̃REH leh R̃(oo)EE-seh-NYOHR KEH kahn-TAH-vah SAW lah R̃AH-mah

Fácteme aquesta embaxata,
FAHK-teh-meh ah kehs-tah ehm-bah-HAH-tah

Y díga olo a mon ami,
EE dee-GAH oh low ah MOWN ah-mee

Que ju ja so maritata,
KEH zhjoo ZHJAH saw MAH-r̃ee-TAH-tah   r̃ = flipped or rolled r.

"Ju Me Leve un Bel Maitín" must be sung in a madrigal style with a light tone and clarity and balance among the parts. Keep a feeling of "one" will help with the style. Slow down only at the cadences.

Evaluation:

Listen to a tape of the choir performing "Ju Me Leve un Bel Maitín." Listen for the following: (*NS 7A, 7B*)

- Beat one as the stressed syllable.
- The dynamic changes indicated by the editor.
- A light madrigal style.
- Good tuning in the open 5th cadences.

Extension:

- Obtain an atlas from your school library to locate the area in Europe from which this song originated. (The northeast corner of Spain, including Barcelona.)
- Ask the students to prepare a report on the part of Europe where Catalan is spoken. (*NS 9B*)

Ju Me Leve un Bel Maitín

(In the Morning I Arose)

For SATB a cappella

15th Century Villancico
Translated and Edited by ROBERT L. GOODALE

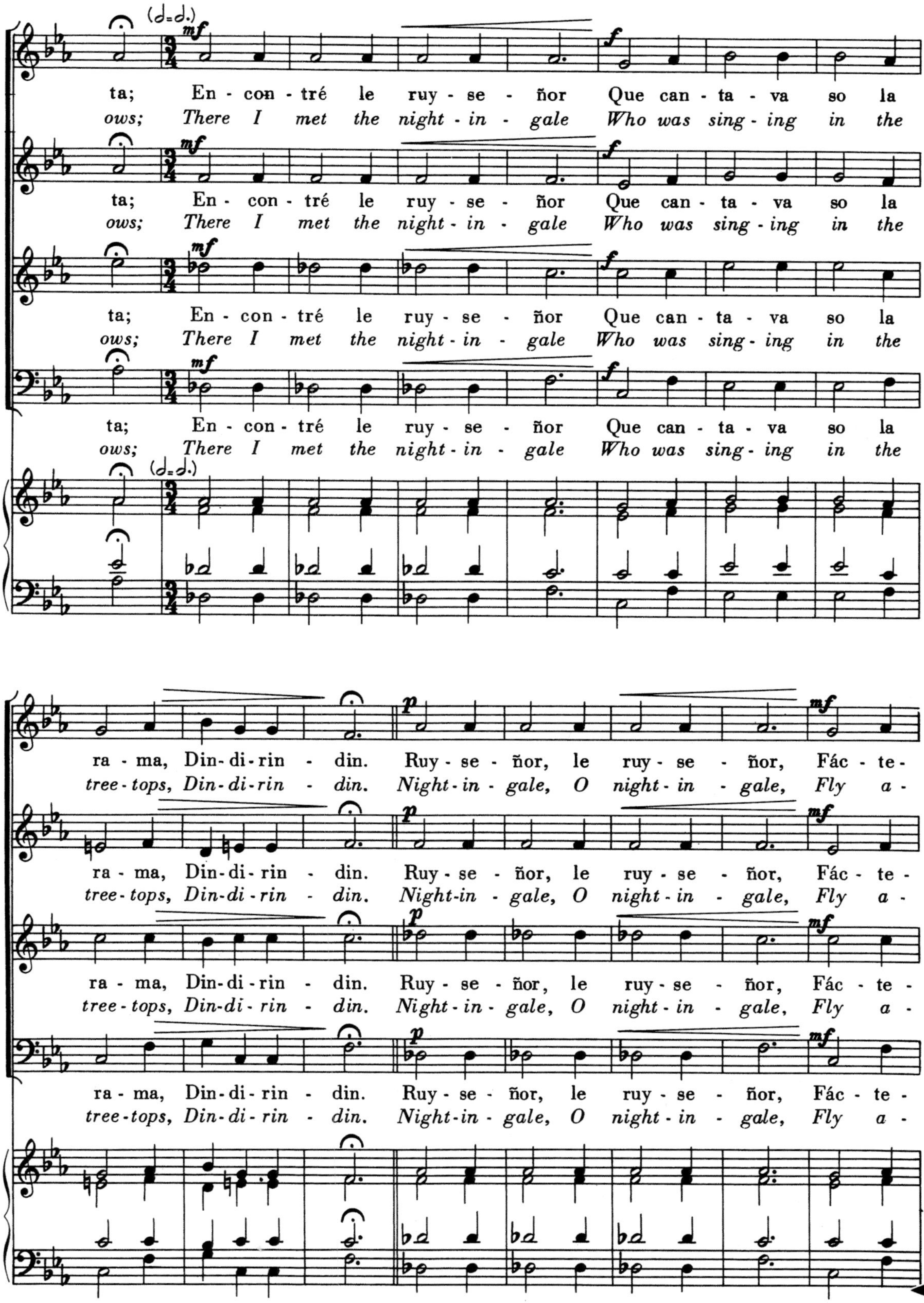

Student Book Page 53

68

Din - di - rin, din - di - rin, din - di - rin - da - ña, Din - di - rin - din.

Din - di - rin, din - di - rin, din - di - rin - da - ña, Din - di - rin - din.

Din - di - rin, din - di - rin, din - di - rin - da - ña, Din - di - rin - din.

Din - di - rin, din - di - rin, din - di - rin - da - ña, Din - di - rin - din.

ritard.

Din - di - rin, din - di - rin, din - di - rin - da - ña, Din - di - rin - din.

Din - di - rin, din - di - rin, din - di - rin - da - ña, Din - di - rin - din.

Din - di - rin, din - di - rin, din - di - rin - da - ña, Din - di - rin - din.

Din - di - rin, din - di - rin, din - di - rin - da - ña, Din - di - rin - din.

Student
Book Page
55

A JUBILANT PSALM

Composer: Emily Crocker
Text: Adapted from Psalms 8 and 67
Voicing: SATB divisi
Key: E-flat Major and E-flat Mixolydian
Ranges:

Meter: 4/4, 5/8, many tempo changes
Form: ABA coda
Style: Sacred contrasting sections, sustained vs. energetic, mostly homophonic

Accompaniment: Piano
Programming: Contest, Concert, energetic opener; Good massed choir number; Good opportunity to teach accented vs. sustained singing

Soprano (div.)   Alto   Tenor (div.)   Bass

Student Book Page 56

A JUBILANT PSALM

Composer: Emily Crocker
Text: Adapted from Psalms 8 and 67
Voicing: SATB

Cultural Context:

This exciting, high-energy piece was written by Emily Crocker in 1991 for a special concert by the Brandenburg Middle School Choir in Garland, Texas.

"A Jubilant Psalm" is written in contrasting styles. The first part is energetic, fast, and accented. Label it "A." The second section (beginning in measure 19) is marked dolce (sweetly) and is to be sung in a soft, sustained manner. Label it "B." Are there any sections of this piece which repeat? Which set of letters best describes the structure of "A Jubilant Psalm" — "AB" or "ABA"?

Musical Terms:

con spirito	(♩ = 138)	(♩ = 152)
f (forte)	*mf* (mezzo forte)	*mp* (mezzo piano)
div. (divisi)	———— *cresc.* (crescendo)	———— (decrescendo)
dolce	*poco a poco*	*piu forte*
syncopated	*molto rit.* (molto ritardando)	Tempo I

Preparation:

Practice the following patterns for rhythmic precision in "A Jubilant Psalm."
1. Steady eighth notes:

2. Syncopated eighth notes:

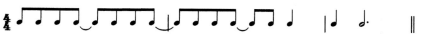

3. Words + syncopated eighth notes:

Sing un - to God __ to His glo - ry a - bove __ all the heav - ens.

Answer to Cultural Context:
ABA

Evaluation:

Can your choir speak the phrase, "Sing unto God, to His glory above all the heavens," precisely together? To check precision, stand in a circle so you can hear each other clearly. Speak the phrase again, emphasizing each beginning consonant. Is each word precisely together and can each word be understood? Repeat this exercise with the sung phrase and with other phrases from the piece.

Objectives:

- The student will develop rhythmic accuracy during performance of "A Jubilant Psalm." (*National Standard* 1E)
- The student will discuss and recognize examples of ABA form. (*NS* 5D)
- The student will explore careers in the field of music. (*NS* 9C)

Historical/Stylistic Guidelines:

Emily Crocker, the composer of over a hundred choral works for developing choirs, is often commissioned to compose a piece for a special group or a special event. Use the following to discuss the different ways composers earn a living:

Submitting works to publishers for possible later publication.

Receiving commissions to compose a special piece for an event or individual.

Receiving royalties on works already published.

For more information about careers in music, see such publications as:

Exploring Careers in Music. (1990), by Paul Bjorneberg, MENC publication.

The Careers in Music Video. (1991), MENC publication.

Essential Musicianship, Book 1. (1995) Hal Leonard Corporation.

Vocal Techniques/Warm-Ups/Exercises:

Warm-up using the following (mm. 19-21) to practice intonation:

- Isolate pitches from rhythm or words and sing on a neutral syllable.
- Hold each chord until it tunes.
- Once the choir knows this chord progression, use it to focus attention on following the conductor by changing the tempo, inserting fermatas, changing dynamics, etc.

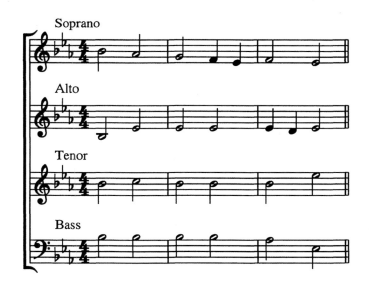

Suggested Sequence:

1. Familiarize students with the musical terms found in this piece as listed in the student text. (*NS* 5C)
2. Begin learning this piece by practicing the rhythm.
   - Practice the rhythmic fragment in the student Preparation.

- Now divide this ABA song into sections and learn rhythms. Rehearse the A sections (mm. 1-15 and mm. 44-53), then B (mm. 19-42), and finally the coda (mm. 54-end).
- When secure, chant the words in rhythm.

3. Stress correct diction while chanting words.

unto = ahn-too, not uhn-too	God = Gahd, not Guhd
earth = careful of too much r	us = ahs, not uhs
that you = that you, not tha chew	the = thah not thuh

the earth = thee earth (long e before a vowel)

the heavens - the hevens (short e before a consonant)

make, face, joy = sing on first (not last) vowel of a diphthong

word stress (HEA-ven not hea-VEN as in m. 8; a-le-LU-ia not a-le-lu-IA as in m. 14)

4. Next, learn the pitches to the B section by using the following procedure:
   - Learn each part separately; then combine all four homophonic parts in mm. 10-34.
   - Rehearse tenors and sopranos together in mm. 35-42 (they have the same part).
   - Rehearse altos and basses together in mm. 35-42 (they are canonic).
   - Combine all four parts.
5. To learn pitches on the A section and coda:
   - Learn by rote unless your choir has had much experience with accidentals.
   - Rehearse each part both individually and in all possible combinations.
6. When all sections are secure, rehearse entire song. Remind students to pay particular attention to the dynamics and phrase markings indicated in the score.

Performance Tips:
- Avoid oversinging on loud passages. This is important for vocal health and good tone.
- Emphasize beginning consonants to give rhythmic drive and intensity.
- Practice a cappella. Don't depend on the percussiveness of the piano for choral energy.
- Make a definite contrast (energetic/accented vs. legato/sustained) between A and B sections.
- Sing in 4 measure phrases, not 2.
- Note the 5/8 section mm. 56-57. Divide the beat of mm. 54-59 into eighth note pulses. Rehearse, reminding the singers to keep the eighth note pulse even and continue marking the eighth note pulse until the rhythm feels natural to the singers.
- Remind the singers that dynamic contrasts and articulation contrasts are essential to a successful performance of "A Jubilant Psalm."

Evaluation:
- Perform the Evaluation from the student page. (*NS 7A, 7B*)
- Tape the choir after they have learned the song. Listen closely for dynamic contrasts, rhythmic precision, balance between parts, and correct diction. Evaluate these categories on a weekly basis to note growth. (*NS 7A, 7B*)

Extension:
- Discuss what "jubilant" means. How many synonyms for the word "jubilant" can the class find? How many songs can they name which have the feeling or intent of "jubilance"?
- Create a piece with contrasting sections (AB or ABA). Use original material or combine songs or pieces of songs students already know. Ask students to explain why they chose to combine the songs they did. (*NS 4A*)

A Jubilant Psalm

For SATB and Piano

Adapted from Psalms 8 and 67

Music by EMILY CROCKER (ASCAP)

Student Book Page 57

74

lu - ia, al - le - lu - ia!

lu - ia, al - le - lu - ia!

lu - ia, al - le - lu - ia!

al - le - lu - ia, al - le - lu - ia!

All na - tions be glad and

Now all be glad and

Now all be glad and

Now all be glad and

Student Book Page 59

75

gra - cious and bless us_____ and make your

gra - cious and bless us_____ and make your

gra - cious and bless us_____ and make your

gra - cious and bless us_____ and make your

sim.

face to shine up - on us,_____ that your

face to shine up - on us._____

face to shine up - on us,_____ that your

face to shine up - on us._____

77

na - tions.

Sing un - to God in the high - est!

na - tions.

Sing un - to God in the high - est!

44 *piu forte*

Sing un - to God to His glo - ry a - bove all the heav - ens!

piu forte

Sing un - to God to His glo - ry a - bove all the heav - ens!

piu forte

Sing un - to God to His glo - ry a - bove all the heav - ens!

piu forte

Sing un - to God to His glo - ry a - bove all the heav - ens!

44

piu forte

R.H.

Student Book Page 63

Sing to His name__ all ye peo - ple who dwell__ on the earth! Al-le-

Sing to His name__ all ye peo - ple who dwell__ on the earth! Al-le-

Sing to His name__ all ye peo - ple who dwell__ on the earth! Al-le-

Sing to His name__ all ye peo - ple who dwell__ on the earth!

lu - ia, al-le-lu - ia, al-le-lu - ia! Al-le - lu - ia!

lu - ia, al-le-lu - ia, al-le-lu - ia! Al-le - lu - ia!

lu - ia, al-le-lu - ia, al-le-lu - ia! Al-le - lu - ia!

Al-le-lu - ia, al-le-lu-ia, al-le-lu - ia! Al-le - lu - ia!

* Sing lower notes only if the upper Tenor notes are out of range.

Student
Book Page
66

JUBILATE! JUBILATE!

Composer: Russian Air, arranged by Joyce Eilers
Text: Samuel Longfellow
Voicing: 3-Part Mixed a cappella

Key: D Major
Meter: 4/4
Form: Strophic
Style: Homophonic hymn-tune
Accompaniment: a cappella

Programming: Concert, contest, or festival

Ranges:

JUBILATE! JUBILATE!

Composer: Russian Air, arranged by Joyce Eilers
Text: Samuel Longfellow
Voicing: 3-Part Mixed a cappella

Student Book Page 67

Cultural Context:
Samuel Longfellow, brother of noted poet, Henry Wadsworth Longfellow, wrote the text used in "Jubilate! Jubilate!" He was born in Portland, Maine, in June 1819 and died there in 1892. Longfellow received his BA degree from Harvard (1839) and the BD (Bachelor of Divinity) degree from the Harvard Divinity School (1846). This hymn was first included in Longfellow's book *Vespers* (1859), a collection of hymns for the Second Unitarian Church. The hymn tune honors the end of another day and the wonder of creation.

Musical Terms:

($\quad$ = 112-120)

mp (mezzo piano)

mf (mezzo forte)

pp (pianissimo)

:|| (repeat sign)

f (forte)

(crescendo and decrescendo)

Preparation:
This piece utilizes 4-bar phrases throughout. Practice this breathing exercise using only one breath. (Repeat as often as needed to perform in one breath.) When you are ready, add the words as found in your music.

The following phrases present a real challenge for Part III, because they are so similar. Can you sing them?

Evaluation:
Record the choir singing this work a cappella (no accompaniment). As you listen to the tape, listen for the following:

1. Can you hear the 4-bar phrases? Listen to make sure that no one is breathing after only 2 bars of music.
2. Is Part III singing the correct pitches in measures: 3, 7, 13, 17, 33, 37, 43, 47, 53, 57?
3. Continue practicing the preparation exercises until you can successfully sing this song with 4-bar phrases and correct pitches.

Objectives:
- The student will develop the ability to correctly shape a phrase. (*National Standard* 1E)
- The student will increase ability to sing in tune while singing close harmony. (*NS* 1E)

Historical/Stylistic Guidelines:

Joyce Eilers—composer, arranger, clinician, and teacher—is particularly well-known for her work with elementary and junior high singers. Her writing and guidelines for 3-Part Mixed idiom revolutionized the middle school/junior high experience. Ms. Eilers received her undergraduate degree from the Oklahoma City University and her masters degree from the University of Oregon.

Review with the students the information found in the Cultural Context section on the student page.

Vocal Techniques/Warm-Ups/Exercises:

To practice tuning chords in close harmony as found in this piece, sing through these exercises daily.

Rehearsal Guidelines and Notes
Suggested Sequence:

1. Familiarize students with the musical terms found in this piece as listed in the student text. (*NS* 5C)

2. This is an excellent piece for students to sharpen their sightreading skills. Teach it by reading the pitches or on a neutral syllable like "noo."

3. Part III consists of three phrases which are repeated throughout the entire piece. Identify them in writing on the overhead, chalkboard, or in a handout as follows:
   - Phrase #1 (mm. 1-4)
   - Phrase #2 (mm. 9-12)
   - Phrase #3 (mm. 13-16)

4. After teaching these three phrases to Part III, direct them to label every phrase in the song with pencil. Each 4-bar phrase will be either #1, #2, or #3 as indicated above.

5. Shift the focus to Parts I and II. Teach their parts together in 4-bar segments. Students will soon discover repetition of material.

6. Combine parts still utilizing sightreading skills or a neutral syllable.

7. Speak the words of the text in rhythm using tall vowels and strong consonants. Note the pronunciation of "Jubilate" is "YOO-bih-LAH-teh" with syllabic stress on the "yoo" and "lah."

8. Teach the final "Amen."

9. Perform the song observing all the dynamic markings indicated in the score.

Performance Tips:

- One challenging aspect of this piece is the chromatic movement in Part III. Extra rehearsal time may be needed to correctly tune the chromatics found in mm. 2-3 (C-natural and C-sharp) and in mm. 14-15 (G-natural and G-sharp).

- Check that the singers are singing in 4-bar phrases with no breath in the middle of the phrase.

- Remind singers to listen carefully for the tuning of the half steps in Part III, as well as the tuning of every chord.

- Ask students to listen to the word stress on the word "jubilate." Stress the syllable "yoo" and "lah" instead of the final syllable "teh."

- Create a rise and fall of each 4-bar phrase with a crescendo and decrescendo. The shaping of the phrases will add musicality to the performance and remove any note-to-note sound. Stress the important words more than the less important words (word stress).

Evaluation:

To check for musical accuracy within each voice part, position one section near a microphone. Direct the entire choir to sing together as the one section is being recorded. Repeat this process for the other two sections. Listen to and evaluate what you hear on the tape. Re-teach as needed. (*NS 7A, 7B*)

Jubilate! Jubilate!

For 3-Part Mixed Voices a cappella

Performance Notes: This piece uses careful voice leading, limited ranges, optimum use of dynamics, and retains the dignity without difficulty that is the essence of this masterwork.

RUSSIAN AIR
Arranged by JOYCE EILERS

Words by SAMUEL LONGFELLOW (1819-1892)

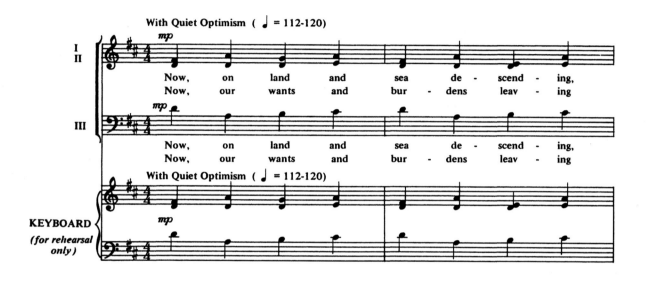

Student Book Page 68

hymn be blend - ing with the ho - ly calm a - round.
cease we griev - ing, at His touch our bur - dens fall.

hymn be blend - ing with the ho - ly calm a - round.
cease we griev - ing, at His touch our bur - dens___ fall.

9 Joyful

*Ju - bi - la - te! Ju - bi - la - te! Ju - bi - la - te!

*Ju - bi - la - te!___ Ju - bi - la - te! Ju - bi - la - te!___

13

A - men! Let our ves - per hymn be blend - ing
Cease we fear - ing, cease we griev - ing,

A - men! Let our ves - per hymn be blend - ing
Cease we fear - ing, cease we griev - ing,

Student
Book Page
69

* Pronounced "you - bih - lah - teh"

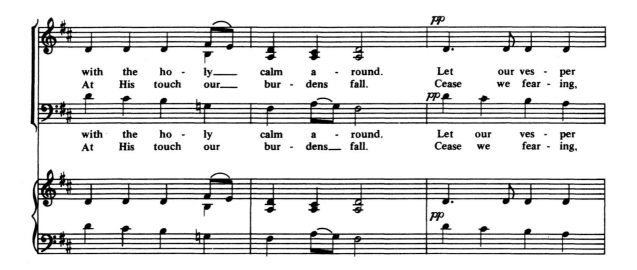

with the ho - ly___ calm a - round. Let our ves - per
At His touch our___ bur - dens fall. Cease we fear - ing,

with the ho - ly calm a - round. Let our ves - per
At His touch our bur - dens___ fall. Cease we fear - ing,

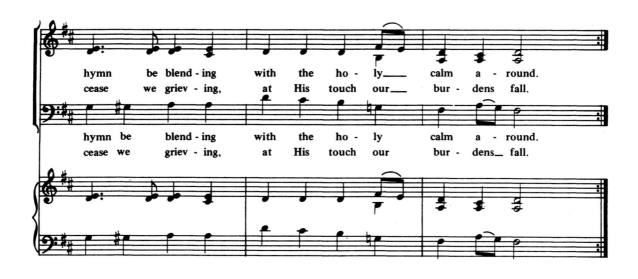

hymn be blend - ing with the ho - ly___ calm a - round.
cease we griev - ing, at His touch our___ bur - dens fall.

hymn be blend - ing with the ho - ly calm a - round.
cease we griev - ing, at His touch our bur - dens___ fall.

21 II

As the dark - ness deep - ens o'er us, Lo! E - ter - nal stars a - rise.

21

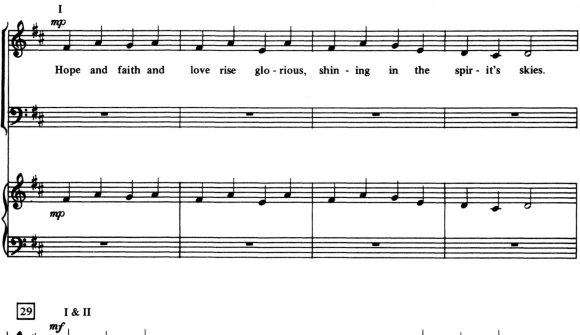

Hope and faith and love rise glo-rious, shin-ing in the spir-it's skies.

29 I & II

Ju-bi-la-te! Ju-bi-la-te! Ju-bi-la-te!

Ju-bi-la-te!__ Ju-bi-la-te! Ju-bi-la-te!__

29

33

A - men! Hope and faith and love rise glo-rious,

A - men! Hope and faith and love rise glo-rious,

33

Student
Book Page
71

89

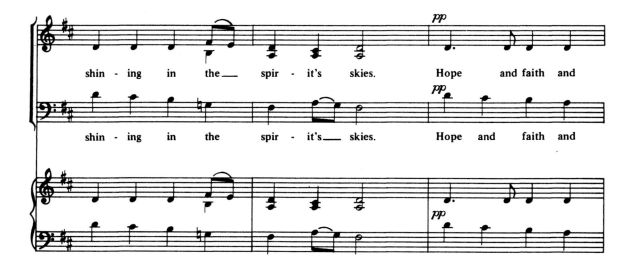

shin - ing in the ___ spir - it's skies. Hope and faith and

shin - ing in the spir - it's ___ skies. Hope and faith and

love rise glo - rious, shin - ing in the ___ spir - it's skies.

love rise glo - rious, shin - ing in the spir - it's ___ skies.

41

Soon as dies the sun - set glo - ry, stars of heav'n shine

Soon as dies the sun - set glo - ry, stars of heav'n shine

41

out a-bove.   tell - ing still the   an - cient sto - ry,

out a-bove.   tell - ing still the   an - cient sto - ry,

49

their Cre - a - tor's   change - less   love.   Ju - bi - la - te!

their Cre - a - tor's   change - less___ love.   Ju - bi - la - te!___

49

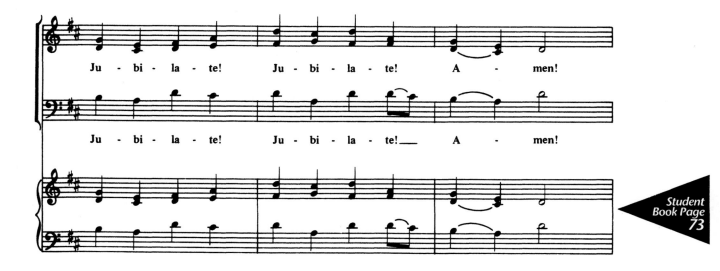

Ju - bi - la - te!   Ju - bi - la - te!   A - men!

Ju - bi - la - te!   Ju - bi - la - te!___ A - men!

Student
Book Page
73

THE MIRACLE OF HANUKKAH

Composer: Emily Crocker
Text: Emily Crocker
Voicing: 3-Part Mixed

Key: C minor
Meter: 4/4
Form: Strophic
Style: Energetic, contemporary, seasonal

Accompaniment: Piano
Programming: Seasonal (Hanukkah) concert

Ranges:

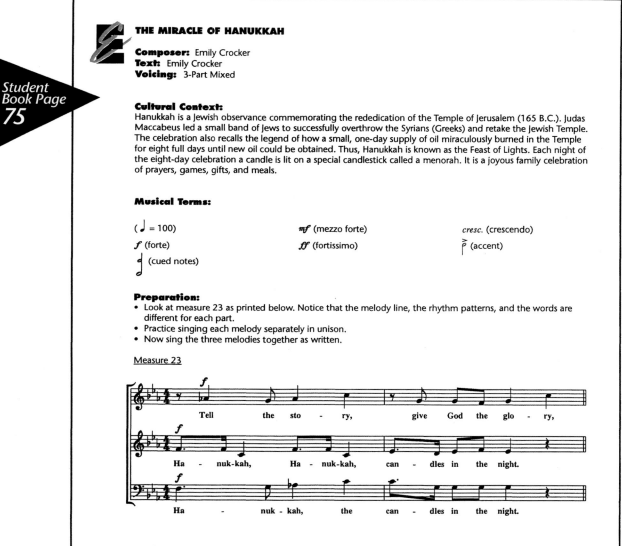

THE MIRACLE OF HANUKKAH

Composer: Emily Crocker
Text: Emily Crocker
Voicing: 3-Part Mixed

Cultural Context:
Hanukkah is a Jewish observance commemorating the rededication of the Temple of Jerusalem (165 B.C.). Judas Maccabeus led a small band of Jews to successfully overthrow the Syrians (Greeks) and retake the Jewish Temple. The celebration also recalls the legend of how a small, one-day supply of oil miraculously burned in the Temple for eight full days until new oil could be obtained. Thus, Hanukkah is known as the Feast of Lights. Each night of the eight-day celebration a candle is lit on a special candlestick called a menorah. It is a joyous family celebration of prayers, games, gifts, and meals.

Musical Terms:

(♩ = 100)

𝑚𝑓 (mezzo forte)

cresc. (crescendo)

𝑓 (forte)

𝑓𝑓 (fortissimo)

(accent)

(cued notes)

Preparation:
• Look at measure 23 as printed below. Notice that the melody line, the rhythm patterns, and the words are different for each part.
• Practice singing each melody separately in unison.
• Now sing the three melodies together as written.

Measure 23

Evaluation:
As you rehearse and perform this selection, can you hear the three separate melodies? Are they equally balanced or is one part too loud? Learn to listen carefully to the other sections of your choir.

Objectives:
- The singer will perform literature of seasonal subject for a formal performance. (*National Standard* 1E)
- The students will listen critically as a participating member of an ensemble, concentrating on the balance of the voice parts. (*NS* 1E)

Historical/Stylistic Guidelines:
Read together the Cultural Context section as found on the student page. Ask the students if they have any more information to add about the celebration of Hanukkah. Ask a student volunteer to read the text of the song. Discuss what the words mean to them. Answer any questions.

Emily Crocker, currently Director of Choral Publications for Hal Leonard Corporation, taught public school music in Texas for fifteen years. She has earned degrees from North Texas University (now University of North Texas) and Texas Woman's University. She has published over one hundred choral pieces.

Vocal Technique/Warm-Ups/Exercises:
To prepare the singers to sing in a minor tonality, practice the following exercise. Ascend by half step to G and back down to F.

Rehearsal Guidelines and Notes
Suggested Sequence:
1. Familiarize students with the musical terms found in this piece as listed in the student text. (*NS* 5C)
2. Start at m. 23 as suggested in the Preparation section on the student page. Teach the three parts separately, then combine.
3. Next teach the 4-measure soli section for each part.
   - Part I - mm. 5-8
   - Part II - mm. 15-18
   - Part III - mm. 33-36
4. The 4-bar phrases following each soli are quite similar. Teach these together as found in: mm. 9-12, mm. 19-22, and mm. 37-40.
5. Review all material learned thus far.
6. Teach the last four measures.
7. Perform the entire piece utilizing all dynamic markings as indicated in the score.

Performance Tips:

- Since this song tells an important story, it is imperative that the words are clearly understood by the audience. Vowels need to be tall and uniform. "Explode" the consonants and go directly to the vowels.
- If diction is unclear, ask students to whisper the words of the song, then sing them. To increase precision and energy, have the students whisper the text in rhythm and exaggerate the consonants.
- Be careful at m. 23 and m. 41 that the higher voices do not over balance the lower voices. All three are equally important and need to be heard.
- This song requires energy in singing.

Evaluation:

Audio tape your choir singing this song. As you listen to the tape, evaluate the following: (*NS 7A, 7B*)

- Correct balance of parts at m. 23 and m. 41. No one part over shadowing another.
- Clear, understandable diction at all times.
- Contrast between the soli sections and the 4-bar phrase following.
- Distinguishable dynamic markings.

Extension:

Encourage volunteers to practice and prepare the solo sections of this song individually. Encourage them to sing it for the class. If possible, have them perform their solos at a public performance.

The Miracle Of Hanukkah

For 3-Part Mixed Voices and Piano

Words and Music by EMILY CROCKER

Lyrics: Chil- dren gath- er 'round now and lis- ten as I sing of

96

Student Book Page 79

100

Student
Book Page
81

101

MUSIC, MOST WONDROUS, LOVELY ART (MUSICA, DIE GANZ LIEBLICH KUNST)

Composer: Johann Jeep (ca. 1581-1644), edited by John Leavitt

Text: Anonymous, German by Johann Jeep, English translation by John Leavitt

Voicing: SATB a cappella

Key: Primarily C major

Meter: 2/2

Form: Strophic with coda

Texture: Polyphonic

Style: Late Renaissance, secular

Accompaniment: a cappella

Programming: Festival, contest, a theme in praise of music; late Renaissance Period piece

Ranges:

Student Book Page **83**

MUSIC, MOST WONDROUS, LOVELY ART (MUSICA, DIE GANZ LIEBLICH KUNST)

Composer: Johann Jeep (ca. 1581-1644), edited by John Leavitt

Text: Anonymous, German by Johann Jeep, English translation by John Leavitt

Voicing: SATB a cappella

Cultural Context:
"Music, Most Wondrous, Lovely Art" was written almost 400 years ago during the *Renaissance Period.* Jeep used a style of composing called *polyphony* in which each voice part begins at a different place, is independent and important, and sections of the music often repeat in a contrasting dynamic level. "Music, Most Wondrous, Lovely Art" is written for *a cappella voices* (without instrumental accompaniment). The words pay tribute to the art of music and the music is written in a light and flowing texture.

Musical Terms:

andante

(𝅗𝅥 = ca. 68)

mf (mezzo forte)

p (piano)

f (forte)

⌢ (fermata)

‖: :‖ (repeat signs)

Preparation:
• A good example of polyphony is mm. 12-16 printed below. Notice how each part has a different rhythm pattern causing the words to fall on different beats in the measure.
• As each section becomes secure in both rhythm and pitch, begin to sing the parts together.

Evaluation:
Brainstorm in small groups and list the popular songs of today which you think will still be sung by choral groups and schools in the year 2400. Make a list of at least five songs. Compare your list with other lists in the class. What qualities must a song possess to last for 400 years? Is it the words, the melody, the organization of the notes on a page, or the challenge of learning it? Why do you feel this song has lasted?

83

103

Objectives:

- The student will develop performance techniques of the late Renaissance Period which includes a cappella polyphony. (*National Standard* 6B, 6C, 9A)
- The student will discuss and recognize similarities and differences between choral styles of late Renaissance and today. (*NS* 6B, 6C, 9B)

Historical/Stylistic Guidelines:

Johannes Jeep (pronounced Yeep) (ca. 1581-1644), German composer and organist, was influenced by the works of Hans Leo Hassler, reputedly one of the greatest German composers of the late sixteenth century. As a child, Jeep sang in chapel choirs and later worked as the chapel master and organist at the court of the Count of Hohenlohe at Weikersheim. He composed over one hundred hymns and psalm settings, but is best known for his collection of thirty-four secular songs which were homophonic songs of simple, folk-like character.

Jeep avoids sameness in his work by exploring rhythmic changes. These changes, found in measure 33, include accented syllables falling on any of the beats, whether weak or strong. This brief meter shift is called hemiola.

Vocal Technique/Warm-Ups/Exercises:

Rehearse each chord to be sure that it is in tune before proceeding to the next. Sing on the neutral syllable "loo."

Rehearsal Guidelines and Notes
Suggested Sequence:

1. Familiarize students with the musical terms found in this piece as listed in the student text. (*NS* 5C)

2. In presenting the material on polyphony found in the Preparation section of the student page, try this suggested teaching sequence:

   - All singers chant or tap the rhythm of the bass part.
   - All singers sing the correct pitches of the bass part on "too."
   - Practice until all are secure on rhythm and pitches.
   - Repeat this process for the tenor, then alto, then soprano parts.
   - Direct each section to sing its own part alone.
   - Sing any two parts together, then finally four parts together.

3. Teach all parts on a neutral syllable. Please note that measures 1-16 are repeated note-for-note in measures 17-32.

4. Add the language.

German: *Musica, die ganz lieblich Kunst ist ehrenwert zu halten.*
Pronunciation: MOO-zee-kah dee gahnts LEEB-leech* koonst eest EH-ř̃ehn-vehř̃t tsoo HAHL-tehn

hat billig allent halben Gunst bei Jungen und bei Alten,
haht BIHL-leeg AH-lehnt HAHL-behn goonst bah(ee) YOONG-ehn oont bah(ee) AHL-tehn

Sie frischt das Herz, welchs leidet Schmerz,
zee fř̃isht dahs hehř̃ts vehlchs* LAH(ee)-deht shmehř̃ts

tut all Unmut vertreiben,
toot ahl OON-moot fehř̃-TŘAH(ee)-behn

lasst traurig niemand bleiben.
lahst TROH(ee)-ř̃eeg NEE-mahnt BLAH(ee)-behn

                            *ř̃ = flipped or rolled r.
              ch = a sound somewhere between ch and sh
        consult German expert for correct pronunciation

5. Perform the piece with all dynamics marking as indicated by the editor.

Performance Tips:

- The tone should be light and free with lots of rhythmic vitality and energy.
- Bring out the moving eighth notes each time they occur.
- To aid in tuning, hold each chord with suspensions until it is in tune, then resolve.

Evaluation:

- Explore the many implications of the Evaluation section as found on the student page. Encourage students to share their lists of songs which they feel will last 400 years. Also, explore possibilities as to why "Music, Most Wondrous, Lovely Art" has survived. (*NS 9B*)
- Are there any similar characteristics among other songs in this textbook which are 300 years or older, such as "Cantate Domino," "Ecce Quam Bonum," "Ju Me Leve un Bel Maitín," and "Psallite"?

Music, Most Wondrous, Lovely Art

(Musica, die ganz lieblich Kunst)

For SATB a cappella

By JOHANN JEEP (ca. 1581-1644)
Edited by JOHN LEAVITT

Student Book Page 84

108

Student
Book Page
87

109

PRAISE THE LORD WITH JOYFUL SONG

Composer: Early American Hymn Tune, arranged by Hal H. Hopson

Text: Based on Psalm 95 (Venite Exultemus)

Voicing: 3-Part Mixed

Key: F Major
Meter: 4/4
Form: Strophic
Style: Hymn style
Accompaniment: Piano

Programming: Concert or Festival; excellent tool for teaching line; good beginning of the year piece

Ranges:

PRAISE THE LORD WITH JOYFUL SONG

Composer: Early American Hymn Tune, arranged by Hal H. Hopson
Text: Based on the Psalm 95 (Venite Exultemus)
Voicing: 3-Part Mixed

Student Book Page 89

Cultural Context:
Hal Hopson, a resident of Dallas, Texas, arranges much sacred music for young voices. This arrangement is based on the early American Hymn tune "Boundless Mercy."

Musical Terms:

rit. (ritardando)   (♩ = ca. 116)   *f* (forte)

ff (fortissimo)   *mf* (mezzo forte)   *p* (piano)

a tempo

Preparation:
1. Three separate melodies are found in this song. Can you identify where each melody begins?

   • Practice each melody in unison.

   • Now sing the three melodies together as they are shown in mm. 65-72. Keep the eighth note patterns very clean and steady.

2. The shape of each line is one of the most important musical elements in "Praise the Lord with Joyful Song." Practice the following exercise paying particular attention to the phrase markings indicated.

1. Loo - loo - loo - loo - loo - loo - loo   loo - loo - loo - loo - loo - loo
2. Praise the Lord with joy - ful __ song; hail the rock who saves us.

Evaluation:
• As you rehearse and perform this selection, can you hear the three separate melodies?

• Are they equally balanced, or is one part too loud?

• Learn to listen carefully to the other sections of your choir.

Objectives

- The student will listen critically as a participating member of an ensemble. (*National Standard* 7A, 7B)
- The student will develop performance techniques including pitch and rhythm accuracy. (*NS* 1E)
- The student will sing with correct syllabic stress. (*NS* 1E)
- The student will perform music in an early American hymn style. (*NS* 1E)

Historical/Stylistic Guidelines:

"Praise the Lord With Joyful Song" is a beautiful hymn arrangement by contemporary composer/arranger Hal Hopson. Mr. Hopson has based this arrangement on the early American hymn tune "Boundless Mercy."

The definition of a hymn has evolved through the years as a poem in strophic form with all verses sung to the same tune. These tunes are often simple and meant for the entire congregation, not just for trained soloists. In 1640, *The Bay Psalm Book* introduced sacred music to the American colonies just two decades after the pilgrims landed at Plymouth Rock. The first book of hymn tunes published in America was James Lyon's *Urania* in 1761. Over 130 such collections were published by 1800. Until the middle of the 1800s, hymn books contained either the first stanza alone or no text at all; therefore, the singer had to use an additional book for the texts. Now, most denominations have their own hymnal, sharing at least half of their hymns and hymn tunes with other denominations.

Vocal Technique/Warm-Ups/Exercises:

Isolate the eighth note runs and use them as vocalises: (Think of descending runs as "going up" in order to keep them in tune.)

1.	ta	ta	ta	ta	ta		ta	ta		ta	ta	ta	ta	ta
----	----	----	----	----	----		----	----		----	----	----	----	----
2.	ha	ha	ha	ha	ha		ha	ha		ha	ha	ha	ha	ha
3.	God		made		all		the	earth		and		sky		
4.	Of -	fer		God	our		grate -	ful		hearts				

Rehearsal Guidelines and Notes
Suggested Sequence:

1. Familiarize students with the musical terms found in this piece as listed in the student text. (*NS* 5C)
2. Review the Preparation section of the student page with the singers.
3. Ask the students to label the three melodies in their music. (Melody A at mm. 5-20, B at mm. 21-36, and C at mm. 41-56) Use each melody as a separate unit for teaching.
4. While learning the notes, remind the singers that each phrase should build in intensity and volume from the beginning to the middle of the phrase, and taper down (in volume only) at the end of the phrase. See the warm-up above.
5. Ask the singers to stress beat one and three and "back away" from beats two and four.
6. As you progress with the notes and rhythms, remind the singers to sing with tall, round vowels. Some examples are: the = thah, above = ah-bahv, us = ahs, and come = cahm.
7. Be aware of all of the "r's" in this text (our, Lord, praise, grateful, worship). Ask the singers to slightly roll the "r's" or use a slight "d" instead. This should help eliminate the "Americanized R."

Performance Tips

- The shape of each line is one of the most important musical elements in "Praise the Lord with Joyful Song." Practice the following exercise paying particular attention to the phrase markings indicated.

- When rehearsing and performing "Praise the Lord with Joyful Song," remind the students to "explode" the consonants and go directly to the vowel sounds in each and every word. With three simultaneous melodies the diction must be crisp and clear.
- Conduct this arrangement in 2.
- Ask the singers to crescendo at mm. 41-42 and at mm. 49-50.
- Pay particular attention to the dynamics indicated by the arranger.

Evaluation:

- As you rehearse and perform this selection, can you hear three separate melodies?
- Are they equally balanced or is one part too loud? (NS 7A, 7B)
- Are the descending eighth note passages in tune? (NS 7A, 7B)

Extension:

1. Ask the students to name other arrangements that they have sung. (Some examples are "Shenandoah" on p. 120 of this book and "Ding Dong! Merrily on High!" on p.16.)
2. Remind the students that this song is an arrangement and ask them if they know and understand the difference between an arranger and a composer. (A composer writes new material and an arranger takes previously written material and adapts it.) (NS 9C)

Praise The Lord With Joyful Song

For 3-Part Mixed Voices and Piano

Paraphrased from Psalm 95

Early American Tune
"Boundless Mercy"
Arranged by HAL H. HOPSON

114

forth their praise; hills re - flect His good - ness. The o - ceans al - so

forth their praise; hills re - flect His good - ness. O - ceans al - so

tell of God; the dry land He cre - at - ed. God made all the

tell of God; dry land He cre - at - ed. God made all the

earth and sky, all cre - a - tion's splen - dor.

earth and sky, all cre - a - tion's splen - dor.

3. Come and wor - ship, kneel be -

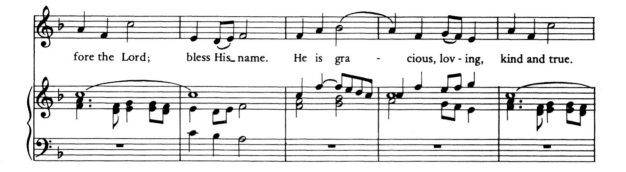

fore the Lord; bless His_ name. He is gra - cious, lov - ing, kind and true.

Bless His_ name. He_ is_ Lord of all.___ We_ are_ His own flock.

Come and wor - ship, kneel_ be - fore the Lord; bless His__ name.

PSALLITE

Composer: Attributed to Michael Praetorius, edited by Henry Leck
Text: English text by Henry Leck
Voicing: SATB a cappella

Key: A Major
Meter: Cut-time
Form: Homophonic
Style: Madrigal
Accompaniment: a cappella

Programming: Concert, contest or festival; excellent tool for teaching languages

Ranges:

▶ *Student Book Page 96*

PSALLITE

Composer: Attributed to Michael Praetorius, edited by Henry Leck
Text: English text by Henry Leck
Voicing: SATB a cappella

Cultural Context:
Michael Praetorius (1571-1621) is one of the most famous composers of the early *Baroque Period*. He is also remembered for his work in music theory and compiling hymns.

"Psallite" is written in two languages, Latin and German. During this time the entire church service was performed in Latin, and most of the sacred music composed was also written in Latin. When Praetorius wrote "Psallite," he was working at a church in Germany. He wrote in Latin and German to please both the clergy and the members of the German congregation.

The style markings and dynamics were all added by the editor, Henry Leck, and did not appear in the original notation.

Musical Terms:

Allegro	*f* (forte)	$\overset{>}{p}$ (accent)
p (piano)	*mp* (mezzo piano)	*pp* (pianissimo)
◁ (crescendo)	*mf* (mezzo forte)	▷ (decrescendo)

Preparation:
Practice saying the Latin and German words in the phonetic pronunciation guide below.

<u>Latin:</u>
Psallite, unigenito, Christo Dei Filio.
SAH-lee-teh OON-nee-JEH-nee-taw KR̄EE-staw DEH-ee FEE-lee-aw

Redemptori Domino puerulo
R̄EH-dehm-TAW-r̄ee DAW-mee-naw poo-EH-r̄oo-law

jacenti in praesepio.
yah-CHEN-tsee EEN pr̄eh-SEH-pee-aw

<u>German:</u>
Ein Kleines Kindelein liegt in dem Krippelein.
Ah(ee)n KLAH(EE)N-es KIHN-deh-lah(ee)n leekt EEN deh(ee)m KR̄IHP-uh-lah(ee)n

Alle liebe Engelein dienen dem Kindelein,
AH-leh LEE-beh EHNG-uh-lah(ee)n DEE-nehn deh(ee)m KIHN-deh-lah(ee)n

Und singen ihm fein.
Oont ZING-ehn eem fah(ee)n

* r̄ = flipped or rolled r.

Evaluation:
Speak the text in rhythm in the following ways, and evaluate both pronunciation and rhythmic precision.

1. All together
2. In sections

Objectives:

- The student will develop proper Latin diction through the use of vowel shapes and syllabic stress. (*National Standard* 1E)
- The student will perform dynamic and tempo changes as indicated by the composer. (*NS* 1E)
- The student will learn and perform music from the early Baroque Period. (*NS* 6B, 9A)

Historical/Stylistic Guidelines:

"Psallite" is written in two languages, Latin and German. During this time the entire church service was performed in Latin and most of the sacred music composed was also written in Latin. When Michael Praetorius wrote "Psallite" he was working at a church in Germany. He wrote in Latin and German to please both the clergy and the members of the German congregation.

Michael Praetorius began his career as an organist in 1604. He spent much of his later years writing his *Syntagma musicum*. This "musical encyclopedia" was a three volume, comprehensive look at the music and style of the age. The second volume was a major source of information on musical instruments of the time. He was also known for his *Musae Sioniae* (1605), a collection of 1,244 church hymns.

"Psallite" was written about the time in history that the settlement of Jamestown, Virginia was founded. Other prominent musicians of the day were William Byrd, Claudio Monteverdi, Orlando di Lasso, and John Dowland.

Vocal Technique/Warm-Ups/Excercises:

The first three notes in each voice part may be a source of tuning difficulties in "Psallite." Practice the following exercise in unison on the neutral syllable "too." This interval drill should help the student with interval singing and listening skills. The purpose of this exercise is to ensure that the singers return to the first pitch each time without flatting.

too - too - too _____   too - too - too _____

Now try to sing the first two measures of "Psallite" also on the syllable "too."

Rehearsal Guidelines and Notes
Suggested Sequence:

1. Familarize students with the musical terms found in this piece as listed in the student text. (NS 5C)
2. Chant the first phrase in rhythm until the singers are very secure with the staggered entrances.
3. Isolate the German section and teach it as a separate lesson. Be sure that the notes are very secure since the language in this section is the most challenging portion of this piece.
4. Remind the students to pay particular attention to the dynamic markings as indicated by the editor in the score.

Performance Tips:

- The tone used in "Psallite" should be light and energetic. A heavy sound is inappropriate for early Baroque music.
- After bringing in each section, conduct "Psallite" in 2. This will help with the rise and fall of the line.
- When teaching the first phrase, pay particular attention to the tuning at m. 3 at the syllable "to." This A major chord can be difficult to tune.
- Make sure that the singers pay close attention to the accent over the word "Psallite" each time it appears. This should have a "bell-like" quality. It can be described as a choral fanfare used to get the audience's attention.
- Pay particular attention to the dynamics and phrase markings as indicated by the editor.
- Take a slight ritard in measure 23 in order to set up the final cadence.

Evaluation:

Speak the rhythm to "Psallite" in the following ways: (*NS 7A, 7B*)

- All together
- In sections

Extension:

Play a recording of other early Baroque choral works.

Psallite

For SATB a cappella

English Text by HENRY LECK

By MICHAEL PRAETORIUS (1571-1621)
Edited by HENRY LECK

Student Book Page 97

Student Book Page 98

125

126

127

SEASON'S GREETINGS

Composer: Traditional Holiday
  Songs, arranged by Joyce Eilers
Text: Traditional Secular Carols
Voicing: SATB

Key: F Major and C Major
Meter: Cut-time, 6/8
Form: Medley
Texture: Homophonic with "fa-la"
  polyphonic section
Style: Holiday, secular

Accompaniment: Piano or
  Instrumental Parts
Programming: Holiday concert or
  festival.

Ranges:

Student
Book Page
102

SEASON'S GREETINGS

Composer: Traditional Holiday Songs, arranged by Joyce Eilers
Text: Traditional Secular Carols
Voicing: SATB

Cultural Context:

This medley can be used as a holiday concert finale and/or audience sing-along. The songs in the medley include: "Deck the Hall," "Up on the Housetop," "Jolly Old St. Nicholas," "Over the River and Through the Woods," and "Jingle Bells."

All of these secular carols should have a light, festive feel. The tone should never get heavy.

Musical Terms:

‖: :‖ (repeat signs)   *sub.* (subito)   *div.* (divisi)

sim. (simile) |1._____ (first ending) |2._____ (second ending)

// (caesura)   𝆑 (forte)   *mf* (mezzo forte)

◁———————▷ *cresc.* (crescendo)   *mp* (mezzo piano)   (no breath)

Preparation:

"Over the River and Through the Woods" is written in 6/8 time. Chant both verses in rhythm.

O - ver the riv - er and thru the woods to Grand-moth-er's house we go._____ The
O - ver the riv - er and thru the woods, oh how the wind does blow._____ It

1.
horse knows the way to car - ry the sleigh thru white and drift - ed snow._____

2.
stings the toes and bites the nose as o - ver the ground we go.

Evaluation:

Create choreography for this medley that reflects a light, festive feel. The movements, like the tone, should never get heavy.

.128

Objectives:

- The student will develop clear diction to convey the meaning of the text. (*National Standard* 1E)
- The student will develop performance techniques including pitch and rhythmic accuracy. (*NS* 1E)
- The student will perform seasonal choral literature. (*NS* 1E)

Historical/Stylistic Guidelines:

"Season's Greetings" is an excellent choral medley of five traditional secular holiday carols. In Medieval times a carol was known as a round dance with musical accompaniment. In form, the carol is made up of a number of regular stanzas with a refrain. Today a carol is widely known as a song for the celebration of the holiday season.

Instrumental parts have been published for "Season's Greetings." This makes an excellent finale for a holiday concert with your school band or orchestra and gives the singers the rare opportunity to perform with a live ensemble.

Vocal Technique/Warm-Ups/Exercises:

This medley contains many short, rhythmic sections such as the "fa-la-la" section in mm. 17-29. For rhythm and pitch accuracy, practice these exercises in the following ways:

1. In sections or small groups
2. All together

1. Ha - ha - ha - ha - ha - ha - ha - ha - ha - ha - ha - ha - ha - ha - ha - ha - ha
2. Too - too - too - too - too - too - too - too - too - too - too - too - too - too - too - too - too

1. Ha - ha - ha - ha - ha - ha - ha - ha - ha - ha - ha - ha - ha - ha - ha
2. Too - too - too - too - too - too - too - too - too - too - too - too - too - too - too

Rehearsal Guidelines and Notes
Suggested Sequence:

1. Familiarize students with the musical terms found in this piece as listed in the student text. (*NS* 5C)
2. Separate this medley into units for teaching purposes.
3. After the notes to each song (or unit) are learned, have the singers practice the same section staccato to give the music a light, rhythmic feel.
4. Make sure that the students understand the first and second endings and repeats in this medley.
5. In mm. 17-29, practice the treble parts alone then add the bass part, and finally add the tenor melody. Make the sopranos, altos, and basses aware that in this section they are an "oom-pah" accompaniment and are secondary to the tenor melody.
6. After each song (or unit) is learned, pay particular attention to the transitions between songs. These transitions can be difficult for the singers, so allow them extra rehearsal time.
7. Rehearse "Season's Greetings" in its entirety. Identify any sections that need reteaching.
8. Remind the singers to pay particular attention to the dynamic and phrase markings as indicated in the score.

Performance Tips:

- This medley should never have a "heavy" sound. These are all secular, festive holiday songs and should be sung with a light, rhythmic approach.
- In measures 12 and 22, be aware of the potential for intonation problems on the descending "fa-la-la" passage in the bass part. Isolate this phrase and use it as a warm up.
- "Up on the Housetop" has an extended range for the tenors. Be aware of the potential vocal problems. Some of the changing voices may want to "mouth" this section rather than "reach" for it.
- Make the students aware of the dotted line phrase markings in m. 32 and m. 44.
- Conduct "Over the River" in 2. This will help with the rise and fall of the line.
- In "Jingle Bells" (m. 72) make sure that the singers hold out the half and whole notes for their full value.
- The 6/8 time signature and close voice parts in "Over the River" can be a challenge for the singer. This section may require some extra rehearsal time.
- Perform "Season's Greetings" with your school band as a holiday concert finale. (Contact the publisher or a music dealer for availability of Concert Band and/or String Pak.)

Evaluation:

- Create some choreography that would reflect a light, festive feel for this medley. The movements, like the tone, should never get heavy. (NS 7A)
- Listen to a recording of the choir singing "Season's Greetings." Do you hear: (NS 7A, 7B)

  - Smooth transitions between songs
  - A light festive tone quality
  - Clear diction
  - Rise and fall to each line

Extension:

Play a recording of any of the songs found in this medley. Ask the students to name other medleys that they have heard or performed. ("Ding Dong! Merrily On High!" on p. 16 of the student book is an example.)

Season's Greetings

(A Holiday Concert Finale)

Deck The Halls • Jingle Bells • Jolly Old St. Nicholas
Over The River And Through The Woods • Up On The Housetop

For SATB and Piano with Optional Instrumental Accompaniment

Performance Note: This is a winter concert finale/celebration of five secular holiday songs
Enjoy!

Instrumental Arrangement by
PAUL JENNINGS

Arranged by
JOYCE EILERS

bright ap - par - el, Fa la la la la la la la la.

Fa la la la.

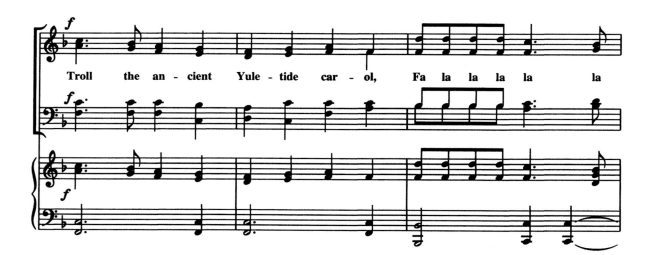

Troll the an - cient Yule - tide car - ol, Fa la la la la la

la la la. La la la la la la.

Fa la la la.

mf (Piano optional to m. 29)

133

la la la.

Christ - mas joys. **Ho! Ho! Ho!** Who would-n't go!

la la la.

Ho! Ho! Ho! Who would-n't go _____ up on the house - top

click, click, click! Down thru the chim - ney with good Saint Nick! Who?

Solo

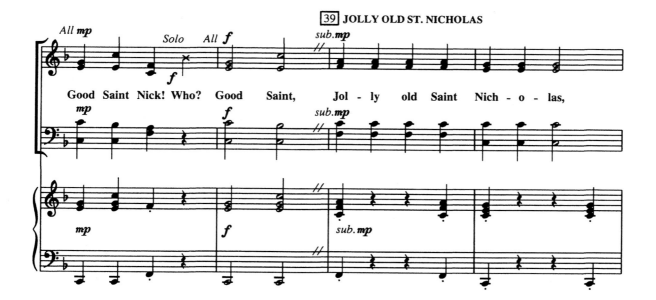

Good Saint Nick! Who? Good Saint, Jol - ly old Saint Nich - o - las,

lean your ear this way! Don't you tell a

sin - gle soul what I have to say!

Student
Book Page
107

47

Christ-mas Eve is com - ing soon; now you dear old man,

tell me what you'll bring for me. Tell me if you

can.

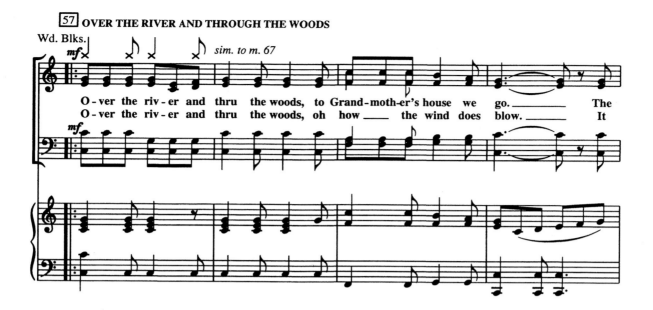

O - ver the riv - er and thru the woods, to Grand-moth-er's house we go._____ The
O - ver the riv - er and thru the woods, oh how ____ the wind does blow._____ It

1.

horse knows the way to car - ry the sleigh thru white and drift - ed

2.

snow._____ stings the toes and bites the nose, as

137

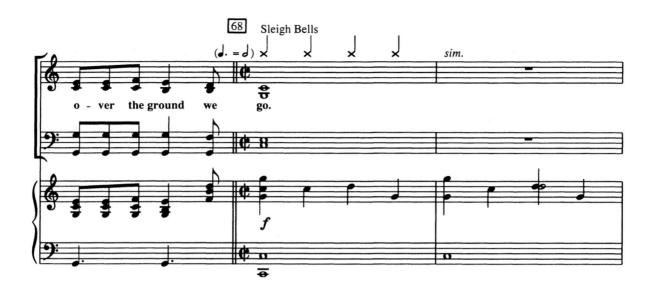

Oh what fun it is to ride in a one horse o - pen

sleigh! _____ one horse o - pen

sleigh! _____

jin - gle bells, jin - gle bells. Jin - gle all the way! Hey!

sleigh! _____

139

SEND DOWN THE RAIN

Composer: Joyce Eilers
Text: Joyce Eilers
Voicing: 3-Part Mixed
Key: A minor

Meter: 4/4
Texture: Homophonic with call and response refrain.
Style: Light, jazz, restless
Accompaniment: Piano

Programming: Concert, pop ensemble; Good tool to introduce jazz style

Ranges:

Student Book Page 112

SEND DOWN THE RAIN

Composer: Joyce Eilers
Text: Joyce Eilers
Voicing: 3-Part Mixed

Cultural Context:
Joyce Eilers was raised on a farm in Oklahoma. This song, dedicated to her parents, compares the restless desert farmland to our own human emotions. She writes that the idea for this song came to her while on a visit to England. However, the lush green English countryside was not the right environment to create the song that she heard in her mind, and it was not until she returned to the dry Oklahoma prairie that the song could be written.

As you learn the song, notice how the music reflects the meaning of the lyrics.

Musical Terms:

syncopation	*rit.* (ritardando)	*cresc.* (crescendo)
mf (mezzo forte)	*f* (forte)	*mp* (mezzo piano)
pp (pianissimo)	*p* (piano)	, (breath mark)
———————— (decrescendo)	𝄐 (fermata)	

Preparation:
Syncopation is a rhythmic pattern that stresses notes on the "off beat." Practice the following syncopated rhythms.

Evaluation:
Can you identify other syncopated sections in this piece? Practice these sections for rhythmic precision.

Objectives

- The student will sing with energy and clear diction. (*National Standard* 1E)
- The student will perform syncopated rhythms with understanding and accuracy. (*NS* 1E)
- The student will sing contemporary choral literature. (*NS* 1E)

Historical/Stylistic Guidelines:

Review the material found in the Cultural Context section of the student page.

"Send Down the Rain" is a good tool for introducing and teaching a pop jazz style. Jazz is one of the only truly American forms of music. Jazz first evolved at the turn of the century in and around New Orleans, Louisana. One characteristic of jazz is the use of syncopated rhythms. "Send Down the Rain" is full of syncopated rhythms. See the student page for more information on syncopation.

The text tells of the comparison of the barren Oklahoma prairie and our own everyday lives. Not only will the rain "wash the dusty sky" and "water the thirsty land," but it will also "soothe my burning soul again."

Joyce Eilers' compositions are consistent favorites of teachers and students across the nation. While her teaching experience spans all levels, she is particularly well known for her work with elementary and junior high singers. Many of her compositions, including "Early One Morning," are standards for this age group. Another example of Joyce Eilers' style is "Jubilate! Jubilate!" found on p. 67 of this book.

Vocal Technique/Warm-Ups/Excercises:

- Practice the excercises listed in the preparation section of the student page.
- "Send Down the Rain" has tricky half and whole step passages in it. Practice the following exercise on the neutral syllable "too."

Rehearsal Guidelines and Notes
Suggested Sequence:

1. Familarize students with the musical terms found in this piece as listed in the student text. (*NS* 5C)
2. Chant the syncopation example found on the student page. Tap the quarter note pulse as the students chant. This will help them identify and master the syncopation.
3. Point out the other like sections (mm. 13-19, mm. 31-37, and mm. 39-45). Have the choir chant these sections. Again, be sure that the singers are tapping the quarter note pulse. Accent the syncopated notes when chanting. (Remind the singers that the syncopated notes are the notes on the "off" or "up" beats.)
4. Make the students aware of the half step intervals in their parts, especially in Part III in measures 13,15,17 and again in the repeated section at mm. 39, 41, and 43.
5. Isolate Part III in the refrain. Point out the descending half step intervals. Remind the singers that a half step is the smallest interval that we sing.
6. The last chord could be tricky for the singers to hear. Isolate mm. 60-62 and learn the parts separately before putting them together. Make the students aware that the piece ends on a jazz chord.
7. Perform "Send Down the Rain" in its entirety. Identify any sections that need re-teaching.
8. Remind the singers to make effective dynamic changes as indicated in the score.

Performance Tips:

- Do not add the piano accompaniment to any section of this song until you feel that the parts are very secure. Before putting the piano with the voices, play through the accompaniment for the class and point out the syncopation in the piano part.
- Keep the tone rich and full until each cut-off and hold each note its full value. Do not taper off the notes at the ends of phrases.
- Accent the syncopated sections.
- The decrease in dynamic at the end of the piece (mm. 54-62) can be very effective. Make use of the entire dynamic spectrum from forte down to pianissimo.
- If the singers are having difficulty perfecting the style of this piece, have them snap on beats 2 and 4 of each measure.
- Work for a steady tempo that is not rushed.
- Use clear consonants to make the words understood.

Evaluation:

- Can you identify other syncopated sectons in this piece? Practice these sections for rhythmic precision. (*NS* 7A, 7B)
- Play jazz recordings for the students. See if by listening, they can identify the syncopated sections in the music. (*NS* 6B, 9B)

Extension:

For more information on the pop/jazz style of choral singing, read Kirby Shaw's book *Vocal Jazz Style.*

For my parents, Mr. and Mrs. Fred Eilers, Mooreland, Oklahoma

Send Down The Rain

For 3-Part Mixed Voices and Piano

Words and Music by JOYCE EILERS

Part I and II or Unison

I live in a des- ert,___ on-ly trou-ble comes___ my way___ as I

try to make_ a liv- in' off___ the land.___

Student Book Page 113

144

You know I'm a be-liev- er,_____ and you know I'm pray-

You know I'm a be-liev- er,__ Oh,_____ and you know I'm pray-

You know I'm a be-liev- er,__ Oh,_____ and you know I'm pray-

- in' hard___ to hear the roll- in' thun- der's might- y sound.__

- in' hard___ to hear the roll- in' thun- der's might- y sound.__

- in' hard___ to hear the roll- in' thun- der's might- y sound.__

Student Book Page 117

147

148

Student
Book Page
119

149

SHENANDOAH

Composer: American Folk Song, arranged by Linda Spevacek
Text: Traditional
Voicing: SATB divisi

Key: D Major, D Phrygian
Meter: 4/4, 2/4
Form: Strophic
Style: Arranged American Folk Song
Accompaniment: Piano

Programming: Concert, contest or festival; audience favorite; good vehicle for teaching sustained, expressive singing

Ranges:

SHENANDOAH

Composer: American Folk Song, arranged by Linda Spevacek
Text: Traditional
Voicing: SATB

Student Book Page 120

Cultural Context:
This familiar American folk song refers to the sorrow early American settlers felt as they left their homes and moved westward to cross the wide Missouri River. Originally "Shenandoah" was a sea chantey sung by sailors longing for home. In some versions of this song, Shenandoah refers to a river (the Shenandoah River in Virginia); in others it refers to a region of the country (Shenandoah River valley); and in still others it refers to the people of the region ("Oh Shenandoah, I love your daughter"). Regardless of the precise meaning of the word, this beautiful song still describes the sadness and loneliness all people, from whatever time, have felt as they prepare to leave familiar places.

Musical Terms:

(♩= 76-80)	*ten.* (tenuto)	*cresc.* (crescendo)
rit. (ritardando)	*a tempo*	***mp*** (mezzo piano)
p (piano)	***mf*** (mezzo forte)	(♩= 92-52)
——— (decrescendo)	Tempo I	*molto rit.* (molto ritardando)

Preparation:
Try this exercise to prepare for the long phrases and pure vowels this piece demands.

1. Breathe deeply and sing a pitch on "oo."
   - Count slowly to 8, 12, or 16 as you sing. Breathe deeply.
   - Try to sing "away you rollin' river" on one breath.
2. A *diphthong* is two vowels sung together. Remember to hold the first vowel and put the last vowel on the very end. It is so short that it is almost unheard.
   - Sing the word "way" and hold it for 8, 12, or 16 beats. Notice that when you sing "ay" you are really singing "eh-ee."
   - Sing the word "wide" and hold it for 8, 12 or 16 beats. "I" in "wide" is also a diphthong and is really pronounced "ah-ee."
   - Try singing the diphthong in "bound" as "ah-oo."

Did you sing the diphthong correctly? Try to sing diphthongs correctly as you rehearse "Shenandoah."

Evaluation:
After you have learned the rhythms and pitches of this song, sing the first two pages and ask yourself these questions as you are singing.

1. Can I sing each phrase on one breath?
2. Can I sing each diphthong in these phrases correctly? Each diphthong is underlined.
   O Shenando' I long to see you, away you rollin' river.
   O Shenando' I long to see you, away, we're bound away, 'cross the wide Missouri.

Objectives:

- The student will develop the breath control needed to support sustained phrases. (*National Standard* 1A)
- The student will correctly sing diphthongs and use tall vowels. (*NS* 1A)
- The student will explore careers in the field of music. (*NS* 9C)

Historical/Stylistic Guidelines:

Discuss arranger vs. composer with singers.

- Have they ever sung any version of "Shenandoah" before?
- How were their versions different?
- Discuss the difference between an arranger (one who develops new settings for songs) and a composer (one who creates the music initially). Do folk songs have a composer? (Usually not, since folk songs are traditionally passed down from generation to generation by word of mouth. We have lost track of most of the composers of folk songs.)

David Ewen, in *All the Years of American Popular Music* speculates that "Shenandoah" may have begun as a ballad "about a trader wooing the daughter of an Indian chief whom he later deserts"(p.29). Later, sailors adapted the melody as a capstan chantey, a song with long sustained melody which was sung as sailors raised or lowered the anchor by slowly and steadily turning a capstan. In one capstan chantey version mentioned by Ewen, a sailor speaks of courting "for seven long years" a girl named Sally who rejects him because he is a "dirty sailor." He finds solace in "drinkin' rum and chewin' terbaccer" as he is bound away "'cross the wide Missouri." The text of the Spevacek arrangement leaves unanswered the question of exactly who or what Shenandoah is.

Linda Spevacek is a well-known choral composer and arranger. After graduating from the University of Wisconsin at Madison, Ms. Spevacek taught music at the elementary, junior and senior high level. In addition, she directed sacred choral music on both the youth and adult levels before becoming a full-time composer and clinician. She currently resides in Tempe, Arizona.

When asked about "Shenandoah," Ms. Spevacek explained that "the emotion felt in this folk song relates to anyone who has had to leave the home they love, their friends, pets, and possibly family. For the singers to emote the feeling of pain and loss is to go beyond the black and the white of the music and create what we know as art."

Other Spevacek works in this series include "The Turtle Dove" and "We Belong."

Vocal Techniques/Warm-Ups/Exercises:

Use the student Preparation exercise as a warm-up to emphasize supported breathing through long phrases every time you rehearse "Shenandoah."
To rehearse potential intonation problems, sing the exercise below.

- Sing on a neutral syllable.
- Hold each chord until it is tuned.
- This exercise is based on mm. 73-79. Directors may want to extract additional exercises to fit problems appropriate for a particular group.

Rehearsal Guidelines And Notes
Suggested Sequence:

1. Familiarize students with the musical terms found in this piece as listed in the student text. (*NS 5C*)
2. Isolate rhythm to the unison first verse on an overhead. Remind students to read the rhythms as written rather than singing them in ways they may have previously learned "Shenandoah."
3. Sing the opening (mm. 5-24) on a blended unison "oo." Add words after pitch, rhythm, and phrasing is secure.
4. Follow the same sequence to learn verse 2 (mm. 27-46). Since the soprano part in verse 2 is identical to that in verse 1, work primarily with alto, tenor, and bass.
5. Follow the same procedure with verse 3.
    • Use the exercise in the Vocal Technique section to assist in tuning mm. 73-79.
    • Learn the rhythms and pitches of each voice part individually before combining parts.
6. Follow the same procedure with the coda.
7. Add piano accompaniment only after all pitches and rhythms are secure. The piano is very expressive, but it does not double the singers' pitches.
8. Remind the singers to pay particular attention to the dynamics, phrase, and tempo markings indicated in the score.

Performance Tips:

• Some tenors may need to sing alto at mm. 27-28 ("O Shenandoah I long to"), mm. 36-38 ("I long to hear you"), mm. 44-45 ("wide Missouri"), mm. 71-end. Write new tenor parts in their music so that tenors see what they are really singing.
• Use cued notes where appropriate to accommodate comfortable ranges.
• Check ranges of changing voice boys at least once a month and be very knowledgeable about exactly what ranges each has so that you can write parts for them. Failing to do so will teach them poor vocal production. OUT OF RANGE = OUT OF TUNE!
• Treat low A's (m. 4 and elsewhere) as pick-up notes. Leaning into the next note (the D) prevents girls from using chest voice.
• Sing 4-measure (not 2-measure) phrases throughout.
• Remind singers to keep the tone spinning with energy across each held note. It takes more energy to sing piano than forte.
• Observe tempo markings, but do not drag. Use much rubato without slowing the overall tempo.
• Use suggestions in the Preparation section to emphasize pure vowels and diphthongs.
• Chart who has the melody on verse 3. Do not let non-melody parts overbalance the melody.
• Pay special attention to the suspensions in verse 3 (especially mm. 59-64). Word stress will make all the difference here, especially on "leave you," and "away." Make this section as intense as possible with sensitive use of rubato and phrasing.
• The dynamic contrasts indicated in the score are absolutely essential for a successful performance of this piece.

Evaluation:

• Read and answer questions on the student Evaluation section with your singers. (*NS 7A, 7C*)

    a. Can I sing each phrase on one breath? (*NS 1E*)
    b. Can I sing each diphthong correctly? (*NS 1E*)

• Ask students to identify other arrangements they have sung. Arrangements in this text include "Didn't My Lord Deliver Daniel," "Ding Dong! Merrily on High!," "Sinner Man," and "The Turtle Dove."

Extension:

Discuss how a song might take on so many different meanings (see student page).
    • Why do people use the same tune again?
    • Ask students to name other arranged songs. They might think of current commercials, currently popular songs which were popular years earlier, or different arrangements of familiar songs.

Shenandoah

For SATB and Piano

American Folk Song
Arranged by LINDA STEEN SPEVACEK

Student Book Page 121

153

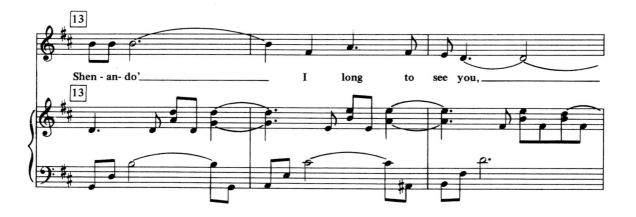

Shen - an - do'_____ I long to see you,_____

cresc.

_____ a - way,_____ we're bound a -

rit.   *a tempo*

- way,_____ 'cross the wide_____

rit.   *a tempo*

_____ Mis - sou - ri._____

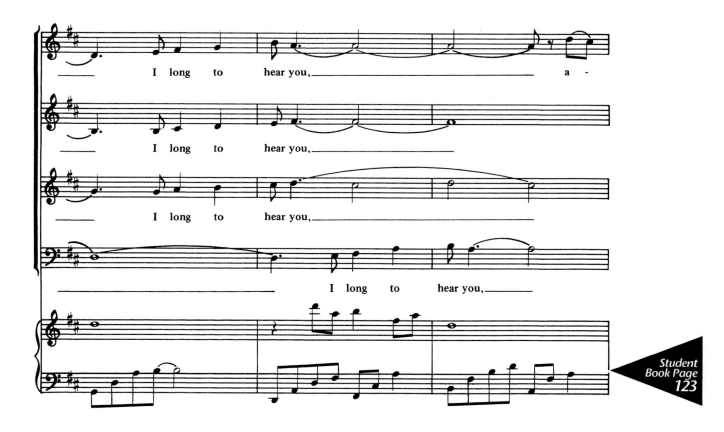

155

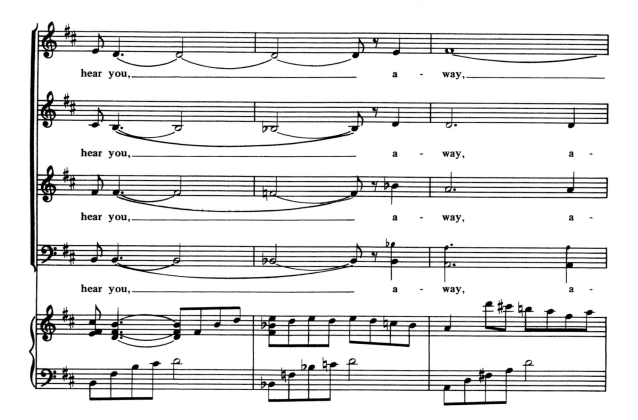

hear you,_____ a - way,_____

hear you,_____ a - way, a -

hear you,_____ a - way, a -

hear you,_____ a - way, a -

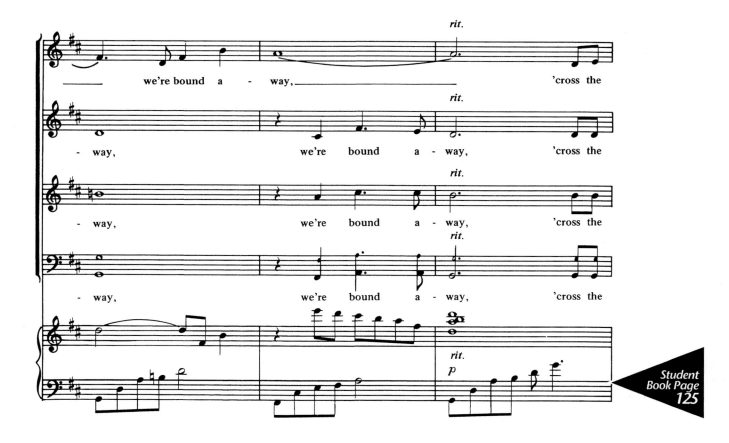

_____ we're bound a - way,_____ 'cross the

- way, we're bound a - way, 'cross the

- way, we're bound a - way, 'cross the

- way, we're bound a - way, 'cross the

Student
Book Page
125

157

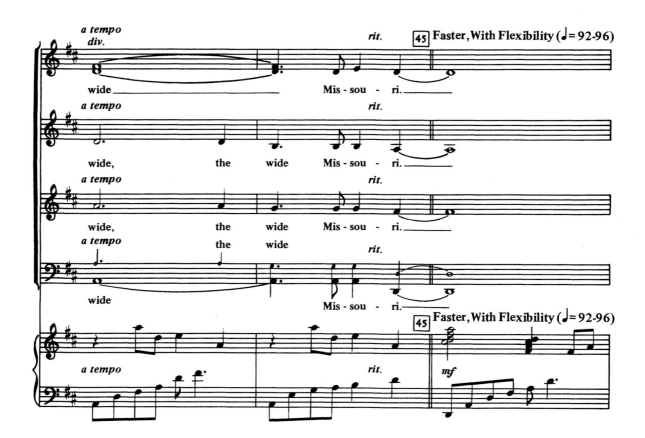

Student Book Page 126

you roll-in' riv - er.___ O my Shen-an -

you roll-in' riv - er.___ O my Shen-an -

riv - er.___ O Shen - an - do'___

riv - er.___ O Shen - an - do'___

- do' I'm bound to leave you,___ I'm bound to leave you, leave you, leave you, a -

- do' I'm bound to leave you,___ I'm bound to leave you,___ a -

___ I'm bound to leave you,___ I'm bound to leave you,___ a -

___ I'm bound to leave you,___ I'm bound to leave you,___ a -

Student Book Page 128

160

Student Book Page 129

161

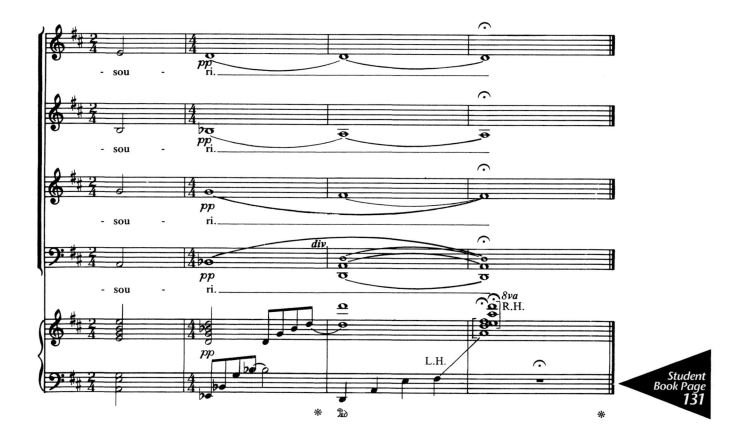

Student
Book Page
131

163

SING PRAISE, ALLELUIA

Composer: Emily Crocker
Text: Emily Crocker
Voicing: 3-Part Mixed
Key: C major, A minor, D major, and G major

Meter: 4/4, 3/8, 2/4, 5/8
Form: ABACA coda
Style: Festive, energetic contemporary piece with sacred text

Accompaniment: Piano or organ
Programming: Excellent festival piece or formal concert

Ranges:

Student Book Page 132

SING PRAISE, ALLELUIA

Composer: Emily Crocker
Text: Emily Crocker
Voicing: 3-Part Mixed

Cultural Context:
"Sing Praise, Alleluia" was written in 1983 by Emily Crocker. This festival piece displays contrast between the rhythmic, energetic opening and ending, and the smooth, *legato* middle section.

Musical Terms:

f (forte)

p (piano)

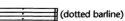 *cresc.* (crescendo)

mp (mezzo piano)

molto ritard. (molto ritardando)

a tempo

(fermata)

(accent)

(dotted barline)

Preparation:
Rhythmic accuracy is important for a successful performance of this piece. The eighth note is constant throughout. You will notice a dotted barline in several places in this piece. The dotted barline indicates the notes to be stressed in the bar, in this case, the first and fourth eighth notes. Find the dotted barlines in "Sing Praise, Alleluia."

In order to learn to keep a steady rhythm, practice this rhythm pattern in two groups:

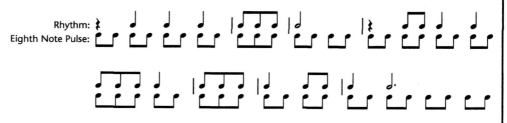

Rhythm:
Eighth Note Pulse:

Evaluation:
To check for accuracy of the ryhthm in the first nine measures of this song, have one half of the class tap a steady eighth note pulse (you may want to use a metronome) while the other half chants the opening text in rhythm.

Are you skilled enough to keep the eighth note constant throughout?

164

Objectives:

- The student will perform "Sing Praise, Alleluia" with correct rhythms especially in the sections with changing meters. (*National Standard* 1E)
- The student will respond appropriately to conducting. (*NS* 1E)

Historical/Stylistic Guidelines:

Emily Crocker lives and works in Milwaukee, Wisconsin. She taught public school music for fifteen years before joining the music publishing industry. This piece was an original composition. Composers have many choices about the type of writing they may wish to do. Ms. Crocker focuses on writing a mixture of compositions with original or borrowed texts and arrangements of pre-existing folk songs or pop tunes.

This piece is a festive, energetic work. The rhythmic accuracy, exaggerated consonants, and dynamic contrasts are essential to the success of this piece. Your students should have great fun with it!

Vocal Techniques/Warm-Ups/Exercises:

- Create a 3-layered overhead transparency.
    - Layer #1 - The rhythm only of mm. 2-9.
    - Layer #2 - The counting patterns that lay under the rhythm.
    - Layer #3 - The words that lay under the rhythm.
- Teach the students how to count the rhythms, then speak the words in rhythm.
- Practice with a metronome set at a slower tempo (♩ = ca.144) then increase the speed. Practice until students are very secure in the rhythm.

Rehearsal Guidelines and Notes
Suggested Sequences:

- Familiarize students with the musical terms found in this piece as listed in the student text. (*NS* 5C)
- Start with the A section (mm. 2-9). After completing the Vocal Technique section above, add the pitches and sing the opening.
- Move to mm. 27-35, which is exactly the same. Review rhythms and pitches.
- The B section (mm. 10-26) is a complete contrast with long, sustained legato phrasing. Teach it in three- and four-bar phrases with a rise and fall of each phrase.
- Allow extra rehearsal time to practice singing the B section with a gradual crescendo over fourteen measures. Measures 22-23 are the peak of the phrase, followed by a *subito piano* in m. 24 and even softer at m. 26.
- Skip to the a cappella transition at m. 35. Create movement in the phrase by leading each longer note into the shorter one that follows. No one should take a breath after the word "earth" in m. 43.
- Teach the last six measures.
- Continue to rehearse the piece, utilizing all the dynamic markings in the score.

Performance Tips:

- The B section (mm. 10-26) should be a direct contrast to the opening A section. Start the phrase softly and gradually build the phrase for thirteen measures, then taper back to *piano*.
- In mm. 42-45 imagine the phrase leading into m. 45. Ask students not to breath or break the momentum in those three measures.
- Students need to feel the steady eighth note pulse underlying the rhythm.
- Sing with energy.
- "Explode" the consonants and move quickly to tall vowel sounds.

Evaluation:

- Lead the class in the Evaluation section as found on the student page. (*NS* 7A, 7B)
- Audio or video tape the rehearsals of this piece frequently. Review the tapes and decide which areas need to be re-taught. Keep the eighth note constant throughout. (*NS* 7A, 7B)

Extension:

Teach your students how to conduct this piece, including the opening nine measures.

Sing Praise, Alleluia

For 3-Part Mixed Voices and Piano

Words and Music by EMILY CROCKER

168

171

Student Book Page 139

SINNER MAN

Composer: Traditional Spiritual, arranged by Roger Emerson
Text: Traditional
Voicing: 3-Part Mixed
Key: D Minor, D Major
Meter: 4/4 Freely, Driving Rock

Form: Strophic
Style: Primarily homophonic arrangement of a Spiritual in pop style idiom
Accompaniment: Piano with optional guitar, bass, percussion

Programming: Concert, beginning of year piece; accessible ranges; Good piece to teach syncopation and expressive markings. Immediate student favorite.

Ranges:

SINNER MAN

Composer: Traditional Spiritual, arranged by Roger Emerson
Text: Traditional
Voicing: 3-Part Mixed

Cultural Context:

"Sinner Man" is an arrangement of a well-known spiritual. It is so well-known that you may already know some version of this song. Spirituals were developed by African American slaves and have become an influential part of American culture. You can probably name many spirituals. You might start with "Swing Low, Sweet Chariot." How many others do you know?

Musical Terms:

Freely (♩ = 69-72)	spiritual	⌢ (fermata)
Driving rock (♩ = 120-138)	♩> (accent)	‾ (tenuto)
♩. (staccato)	hushed	*p* (piano)
mf (mezzo forte)	*f* (forte)	*cresc.* (crescendo)
syncopated	♩ ♩ (no breath)	

Preparation:

This arrangement of "Sinner Man" is interesting because it asks the choir to change moods for each verse. Each section is quite different. Look at your music and find how each section is changed. Can you answer just by looking at the music, or do you need to hear it first?

Introduction (*Oh sinner man,* mm. 1-8)

Verse 1 (*Run to the rock,* mm. 12-19)

Verse 2 (*Run to the sea,* mm. 20-28)

Verse 3 (*Oh sinner man, should a been a prayin',* mm. 28-37)

Verse 4 (*Oh sinner man, where you gonna run to,* mm. 38-end)

Evaluation:

After you have learned the pitches and rhythms of this song, make a copy of the following graph showing how each verse of "Sinner Man" should be performed. Write one word in each square.

	Slow/Fast	Loud/Soft	Syncopated/Not Syncopated
Intro			
Verse 1			
Verse 2			
Verse 3			
Verse 4			

Now sing the song. Are you performing each verse exactly as indicated in the music?

(Answers to Cultural Context)

Swing Low Sweet Chariot
Steal Away
Soon I Will Be Done
Ride the Chariot
Ezekial Saw the Wheel

(Answers to Preparation)

Introduction: slower, softer, not syncopated

Verse 1: faster; louder; syncopated

Verse 2: faster (or stays the same); louder (or stays the same); syncopated

Verse 3: slower (or stays the same); softer; syncopated

Verse 4: faster; louder; syncopated

Objectives:

- The student will perform dynamic and tempo changes as indicated by the composer. (*National Standard* 1E)
- The student will perform syncopated rhythms with understanding and accuracy. (*NS* 1E)
- The student will perform contemporary choral literature. (*NS* 1E)

Historical/Stylistic Guidelines:

"O Sinner Man" is a style of spiritual known as call and response designed to be sung first by a soloist and then answered by a group of singers. The harmony is especially important in this spiritual. As David Ewen remarks in *All the Years of American Popular Music*, "Unlike many other American folk songs, the spiritual was created not by an individual, but by groups; it was meant to be sung chorally, not solo. Consequently—almost unique in American folk music—the interest lies not only in the melody, but in the harmony" (p. 32).

Roger Emerson, the arranger of "O Sinner Man," is one of the most widely performed choral composer/arrangers in America today with over 375 titles in print, and 9 million copies in circulation. He received his degree in choral music education from Southern Oregon State College and taught for seven years in the Mt. Shasta Public School System. He concluded his teaching career by conducting the vocal jazz program at the College of the Siskiyous and now devotes full time to writing and consulting. He currently lives and composes in Mt. Shasta, California. Other Emerson works in this volume include: "Didn't My Lord Deliver Daniel" and "Good Timber Grows."

Vocal Technique/Warm-Ups/Exercises:

Introduce syncopation by using the following exercise as a warm-up:

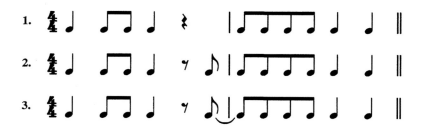

- Add the words "run to the rock, rock won't you hide me" under each example.
- Remind students how much energy and interest is added by performing off the usually accented beat. Ask them to find places in "O Sinner Man" in which the above pattern appears. (mm. 12-13, 14-15, 16-17, 20-21, 22-23, 24-25, 28-29, 30-31, 32-33, 38-39, 40-41, 42-43)

Rehearsal Guidelines and Notes
Suggested Sequence:

1. Familiarize students with the musical terms found in this piece as listed in the student text. (*NS* 5C)
2. Introduce syncopation using the warm-up above. Simplify rhythms by gradually adding ties to teach potentially confusing sections (such as mm. 18-19).

3. When teaching this song to inexperienced singers, teach the rhythm first by putting only rhythm on the overhead. Isolating rhythm from pitches, accompaniment, words, etc. allows novice readers to focus only on rhythm.

4. Then teach the pitches (use numbers, syllables, or letter names), also using an overhead. Write the pitches with quarter notes only, then add pitches in the correct rhythm.

5. Read pitches and rhythms together from the score; add the text when the notes are secure.

6. Add piano accompaniment only after pitches and rhythms are secure.

7. Remind the students to pay particular attention to the dynamics and tempo markings indicated in the score. Use the student Preparation as an activity to emphasize markings in the score.

Performance Tips:

• Know the ranges of your boys. Use the notated tenor part (or write in one of your own) where appropriate so that boys are not singing out of range. OUT OF RANGE = OUT OF TUNE!

• Use the introduction to teach how to follow the conductor. Vary your interpretation as singers follow.

• Add energy through piano or percussion after the singers thoroughly know the song.

• Allow plenty of rehearsal time if you are choosing to use a student percussionist because junior high drummers may have difficulty playing softly at this stage in their development. This piece also works well without percussion.

• Hold out pitches for their full value (as in mm. 8-9, basses on m. 20). Insist on breath support.

• Emphasize precise diction ("won't you," not "won chew").

• Remind singers not to slide on mm. 39-40 (beat 4 to 1).

• Rehearse the ending rhythm carefully because it is the only different pattern. Novice singers may tend to put "day" on beat 1 instead of on the second half of beat 1.

• Altos may experience difficulty finding their pitch in m. 20. To assist them, ask the altos to sing the bass pitches in m. 20 up an octave and then hold the alto note. The exercise would thus be A- F-E-D-F (hold). Repeat until the pattern is secure in their ears. Then switch to words: "Run to the sea Sea (hold)." Finally, ask the altos to mentally sing the bass part and enter on their on their own pitch; hold that pitch (alto F.) Repeat this process until the F is secure, then try adding the basses and have the altos hold their opening pitch (F). Isolating difficult sequences and repeating them until they are absolutely secure is often an effective way of solving potential pitch inaccuracies.

Evaluation:

• Use the Evaluation in the student text to emphasize knowledge of contrasting sections. (NS 7A, 7B)

• Ask singers to find each term under Musical Terms in their copies and to look up any terms they do not know in the glossary. Use "Sinner Man" as a vehicle to teach the expressive terms to be emphasized the rest of the year. (NS 5C)

• Tape the entire choir singing a specific verse. Let the singers listen and critique their progress on rhythmic precision and correct notes. Use only short examples to build concentrated listening. Encourage teamwork. (NS 7A)

Extension:

Suggest that students explore characteristics of spirituals by comparing "Sinner Man" with another spiritual in this book, "Didn't My Lord Deliver Daniel," p. 8 of the student text. (NS 6B)

(Common characteristics might include syncopation, driving rhythms, religious texts, slow introductions, same arranger, minor keys, etc.)

Sinner Man

For 3-Part Mixed Voices and Piano with Optional Rhythm Section

Spiritual
Adapted and Arranged by ROGER EMERSON

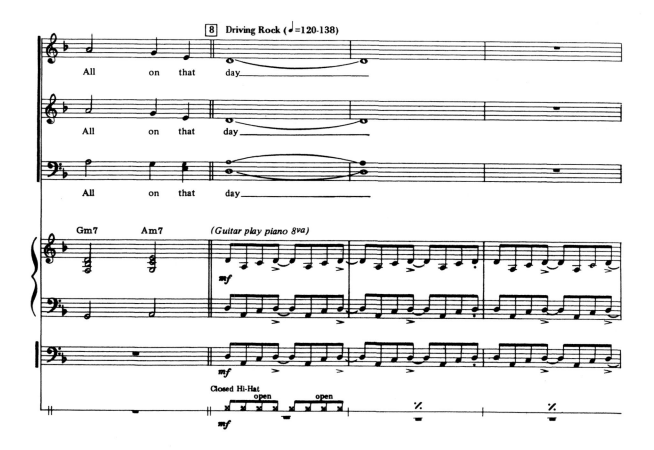

Student
Book Page
142

177

179

Student Book Page 145

Student
Book Page
146

181

182

THE TURTLE DOVE

Composer: Traditional English Folk Song, arranged by Linda Spevacek

Text: Traditional

Voicing: 3-Part Mixed

Key: G minor

Ranges:

Meter: 4/4

Form: Strophic

Style: Expressive American Folk Song

Accompaniment: Piano with Optional Flute

Programming: Concert or festival; limited ranges; good for both beginning and more advanced choirs

Student Book Page 148

THE TURTLE DOVE

Composer: Traditional English Folk Song, arranged by Linda Spevacek
Text: Traditional
Voicing: 3-Part Mixed with Flute (optional)

Cultural Context:
This beautiful folk song describes the sorrow of leaving a loved one. That pain is compared with the sound of a turtle dove mournfully cooing in the distance. The song is a promise to return ("though I roam ten thousand miles") and a promise to remain faithful ("till the stars fall from the sky"). Like most folk songs, "The Turtle Dove" has been handed down from generation to generation.

Read the words to yourself and enjoy singing the beautiful melody that goes with them.

Musical Terms:

unison	*a tempo*	*rit.* (ritardando)
molto rit. (molto ritardando)	*mp* (mezzo piano)	*f* (forte)
(fermata)	*p* (pianissimo)	// (caesura)
(tenuto)		

Preparation:
A. Having enough breath to sing through each phrase may be a challenge in this piece. To prepare, try this exercise. You may have to repeat it several times.

   • Breathe deeply and read each line slowly on one breath.

   Fare you well my dear I must be gone and leave you for awhile.

   If I roam away I'll come back again tho' I roam ten thousand miles my dear.

B. Correct diction of words which contain diphthongs may be a problem in this piece. A diphthong is two vowels sung together to make one continuous sound.

1. Sing and hold "i" words (while, mile, right) on a pitch .

   • Notice that when you sing the "i" of "while" you are really singing "AH-(ee)."

   • When singing in English, the last vowel in a diphthong is put at the very end. It is so short that it is almost not heard.

2. Circle each word in "The Turtle Dove" that has an "i" sound. The circles will remind you to sing the diphthong correctly.

Evaluation:
After you have learned the rhythms and pitches of this song, pay special attention to how you personally are singing "i" diphthongs. Are you singing them correctly? Are you holding the "ahhhh"? Is there too much "ee"? As you sing other songs, pay attention to how accurately you are singing "i" diphthongs.

Objectives:

- The student will develop the posture and breath control needed to support sustained phrases. (*National Standard* 1A)
- The student will correctly sing diphthongs and tall vowels. (*NS* 1A)
- The student will perform traditional choral literature. (*NS* 1E)

Historical/Stylistic Guidelines:

Linda Spevacek is a highly sought choral composer and arranger. After graduating from the University of Wisconsin at Madison, Ms. Spevacek taught music at the elementary, junior and senior high level. In addition, she directed sacred choral music on both the youth and adult levels before becoming a full time composer and clinician. She currently resides in Tempe, Arizona. Other Spevacek works in this volume include "Shenandoah" and "We Belong."

When asked about the writing of "The Turtle Dove," Ms. Spevacek replied that "the haunting minor melody and text depict the sadness and pain of love. I tried to capture the essence of the text with loneliness, but warmth in the piano and flute. The rest I left to the singer . . . to color the words and paint with tone."

American folk songs are most frequently of foreign origin, but the tunes were transformed by the American experience. Folk songs accompanied early Americans, but each area of the country or type of work produced its own melodies. Folk songs included the songs of vendors who sold their wares in the city streets; lumber folk songs describing the rugged life of the lumberjack; sea chanteys, work songs sung in the rhythm of a task; the "lonesomes" of Appalachia; variations on English ballads; folk songs of the western migration; and of course, the spirituals of slavery. An interesting discussion of how the variety of folk songs developed into popular commercial music today may be found in David Ewen's *All the Years of American Popular Music.* Other notable folk song collections include those of Alan Lomax, Carl Sandburg, and John Jacob Niles.

Vocal Technique/Warm-Ups/Exercises:

1. Perform the breathing exercise on the student Preparation section.
2. Before performing the diphthong exercise in the Preparation section of the student page, practice the following positive and negative diphthong examples:

   - Instruct the choir to hold the word "right" on a comfortable pitch.
   - Emphasize that "I" has two vowel sounds (AH-ee). Many people are unaware of the presence of two vowel sounds unless they are told.
   - Have the chorus sing the "ah" and don't sing the "ee" until the "t" on the cutoff. Practice these distinctions several times before attempting words with less precise ending consonants (while, mile, mine).
   - Repeat until the singers are precise, then rehearse the diphthong exercise on student page.

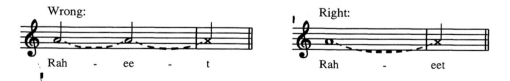

Rehearsal Guidelines and Notes
Suggested Sequence:

1. Familiarize students with the musical terms found in this piece as listed in the student text. (*NS* 5C)
2. Teach verse 1 (unison) to all singers. Each singer eventually has that melody.
3. Teach rhythms, then pitches to one verse at a time.
4. Teach the Coda last because it may be the most difficult section to tune.

Performance Tips:

- Sing 4-measure phrases, not 2-measure, throughout. Stagger breathing if necessary.
- This is a good piece for working on tall vowels and good diction.

come = cahm not cuhm	a while = ah-while not uh-while
love = lahv not luhv	the = thah not thuh
from = frahm not fruhm	thou = thah(oo) (emphasize ah)

generally avoid all "uh" sounds by raising the soft palate

- Hold all notes to their full value; maintain energy on held notes (as mm. 17-18 and elsewhere).
- Verse 2 begins the harmony. Check that all parts are present in m. 22 where the first harmony occurs and again on m. 23 where the first three-part section occurs.
- Tune unison notes approached from harmony (e.g. m. 26 "lad I" and elsewhere).
- Rehearse the dissonance of the coda carefully. The following exercise may help:

- Remind the students to pay particular attention to the dynamics and phrase markings indicated in the score. These will make an important expressive difference in "Turtle Dove."

Evaluation:

- Check student pronunciation of diphthongs by reading and discussing the student Evaluation. (*NS 7A, 7B*)

Extension:

- Ask students to create a story which ends with the singing of "The Turtle Dove." Who is the character who says "I must be gone"? Who is being left behind? Why? What has happened to bring them to this point?
- Your singers may want to make their story into a play. One possibility is to write a story which would include several folk song arrangements. The chorus might then present the play (or narration) during a concert of folk songs. (*NS 8A*) Additional American folk song and spiritual arrangements in this series include:

Didn't My Lord Deliver Daniel	Children Go Where I Send Thee
Sinner Man	Drill Ye Terriers
Shenandoah	This Train
Cripple Creek	Aura Lee
Charlotte-town	Crawdad Hole
Songs of a Starry Night	Mary Had a Baby
Drunken Sailor	Blow Ye Winds

The Turtle Dove

For 3-Part Mixed Voices and Piano with Optional Flute

Traditional English Folk Song
Arranged by LINDA SPEVACEK

Student
Book Page
149

186

while. If I roam a - way I'll come back a - gain, tho' I

roam ten thou - sand miles, my dear, tho' I roam ten thou - sand

miles.

The Turtle Dove

For 3-Part Mixed Voices and Piano with Optional Flute

FLUTE

Traditional English Folk Song
Arranged by LINDA SPEVACEK

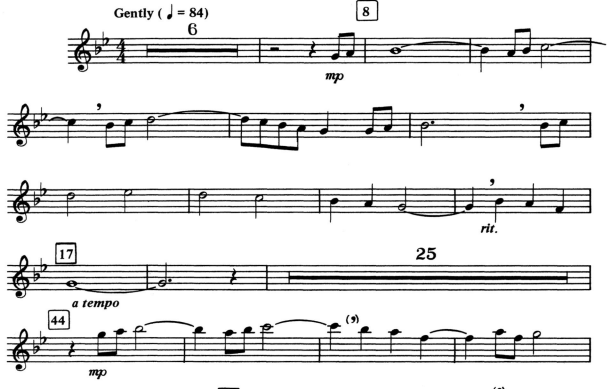

196

WE BELONG

Composer: Linda Spevacek
Text: Linda Spevacek
Voicing: SATB

Key: G Major
Meter: Cut-time
Form: Strophic
Style: Pop style idiom
Accompaniment: Piano

Programming: Concert, easy beginning mixed piece, good massed choir choice. Two-part and 3-part mixed versions are compatible with the SATB printed here.

Ranges:

Student Book Page 160

WE BELONG

Composer: Linda Spevacek
Text: Linda Spevacek
Voicing: SATB

Cultural Context:
The words to this song have an extremely important message. Read them to yourself before you begin learning the song.

Verse
Some people you and I may know are born with a diff'rent skin.
They live in many diff'rent ways in places we've not been.
But it matters not in this great big world, whether they are black, yellow, red or white,
No it matters not in this great big world, together in spirit we are all as one.

Chorus
Oh, we belong and you belong together in one family,
Let the world now celebrate and live in perfect harmony.
We belong and you belong together in one family.
Here we stand, united we stand, strong in spirit we are all as one.

Verse
If ev'ryone would take the time to care for his fellow man.
And always keep on trying to give help where he can,
Then a better world would be made each day, so take a stand, lend a helping hand,
Then a better world would be made each day, together in spirit we are all as one.

Chorus Repeats

Musical Terms:

unis. (unison)   *mf* (mezzo forte)   *f* (forte)

Preparation:
Practice this rhythm pattern before you sing the song.

① (rhythm notation)

② (rhythm notation)

Now look at measure 25. What do you notice about the rhythm there? How many times does that pattern appear in this song? Reading a new song is much easier when you notice repeated patterns.

Evaluation:
An important part of being a performer is the ability to express your feelings to an audience. After you have learned "We Belong," videotape your choir singing this song. Does your face express what the song means to you? Write an essay discussing what the words of "We Belong" mean to you.

(Answer to student Preparation)
Rhythm of m. 25 is the same as the rhythm in the exercise. The pattern ♩♫♩♩ appears 32 times throughout "We Belong."

Objectives:

- The student will sing expressively by using appropriate facial expressions. (*National Standard* 1E)
- The student will use clear diction to convey meaning of text. (*NS* 1A)
- The student will work effectively with others as a responsible team member by creating original choreography in groups. (*NS* 7A)

Historical/Stylistic Guidelines:

Linda Spevacek wrote this piece and dedicated it to her "friend and inspiration, John Jacobson." John Jacobson is a singer, choral director, dancer, choreographer, and organizer of the America Sings! project in which choirs raise money for homeless children by performing across the country.

When asked about the composing of "We Belong," Ms. Spevacek replied that every year she writes "a 'signature' song—a piece with a message from my heart and my own experience. The more I traveled, the more I saw that all people's true spirits are good, everyone is valuable. This piece is dedicated to my good friend, John Jacobson, because he also truly believes and lives that belief."

Vocal Technique/Warm-Ups/Exercises:

Tonal Preparation: Use the following as a warm-up, so that when singers encounter the harmony in the first four bars of the chorus (mm. 25-28 and throughout), they will sing it more easily.

- Sing on a neutral syllable ("doo" or "too").
- Hold each chord until it tunes.

Rehearsal Guidelines and Notes
Suggested Sequence:

1. Familiarize students with the musical terms found in this piece as listed in the student text. (*NS* 5C)
2. Use the exercise on the student page to prepare for the rhythms of "We Belong."
3. Teach the chorus first (mm. 25-43).
4. Teach the rhythm by writing the rhythm on the overhead (isolated from words and pitches).
5. Chant the rhythm using words.
6. Sightread the pitches of each voice part separately. (You may want to write each part out separately on the overhead because it may be confusing for novice readers to see two notes on a staff at once.)
7. Rehearse parts in all possible combinations.
8. Ask singers to compare mm. 65-82 with mm. 25-43. (They are identical.) Do not assume that singers notice repetition of parts.
9. Follow the same procedure to teach the coda and, finally, the unison verses.
10. Identify and rehearse sections that need re-teaching.
11. Remind the students to pay particular attention to the dynamics indicated in the score.

Performance Tips:

- Note that the bass and soprano are in unison throughout the entire piece except for mm. 5-12.
- Remind the singers to hold half notes full value without gasping at the ends of phrases.
- Emphasize beginning and ending consonants for clarity of words.
- Sing four-measure rather than two-measure phrases.
- Check ranges of changing voice boys. High tenors may sing melody during mm. 5-12 or even mm. 5-22 if it is more appropriate for their ranges. Rephrase the comment: "Tenors sing with the girls." to "Tenors sing the melody line."
- Write in any changes in the tenor parts so singers see the notes they are singing. An example appears below. Note that tenors are merely doubling the alto, but their part is written in bass clef. A little teacher time spent writing out parts will pay off later in increased reading skills.

Evaluation:

- Videotape the choir and evaluate facial expression as specified on the student page. (NS 7A, 7B)

  Hints for taping: Videotape the choir standing in rows (preferably on risers) while rehearsing "We Belong." Tape a brief close-up of each singer on the front row then move the front row to the back and bring the next row up. Continue this cycle. Show the tape to the choir after viewing it yourself to check for any potential problems that you did not see while you were taping. Emphasize that facial expression, energy, and movement of the mouth make for better singing.

- Keep the video and do the same exercise periodically throughout the year. At the end of the year show the choir their first tape and let them see how much improvement they have made as singers. (NS 7A, 7B)

Extension:

Suggest that students design their own choreography to "We Belong."

We Belong

For SATB and Piano

Words and Music by LINDA SPEVACEK

201

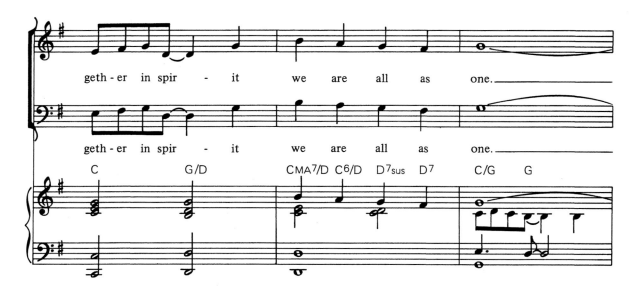

geth - er in spir - it we are all as one._____

geth - er in spir - it we are all as one._____

C   G/D   CMA⁷/D C⁶/D D⁷sus D⁷   C/G   G

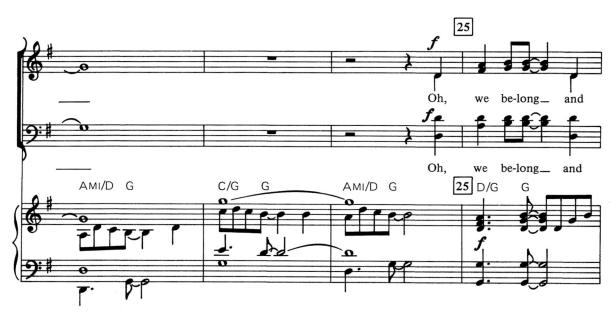

Oh, we be-long___ and

Oh, we be-long___ and

AMI/D G   C/G G   AMI/D G   **25** D/G G

you be-long___ to - geth - er in one fam - i - ly,___

you be-long___ to - geth - er in one fam - i - ly,___

D/F♯   G/F♯   C/E EMI⁷ G/D   C   G/B

let the world___ now cel - e - brate___ and live in per - fect

let the world___ now cel - e - brate___ and live in per - fect

C   G/B   C   G/B   A MI   E MI/B   C6   C

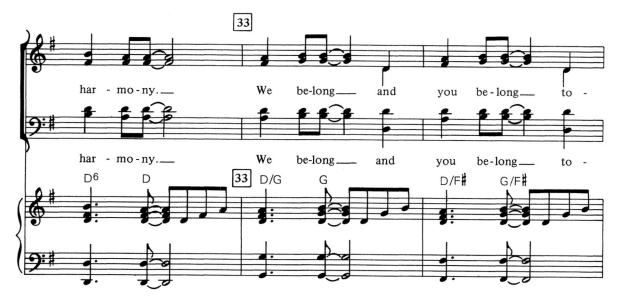

33

har - mo - ny.___   We be-long___ and you be-long___ to -

har - mo - ny.___   We be-long___ and you be-long___ to -

D6   D   **33**   D/G   G   D/F#   G/F#

geth - er in one fam - i - ly.___   Here we stand,___ u -

geth - er in one fam - i - ly.___   Here we stand___ u -

C/E   E MI7   G/D   C   G/B   C   G/B

Student
Book Page
164

203

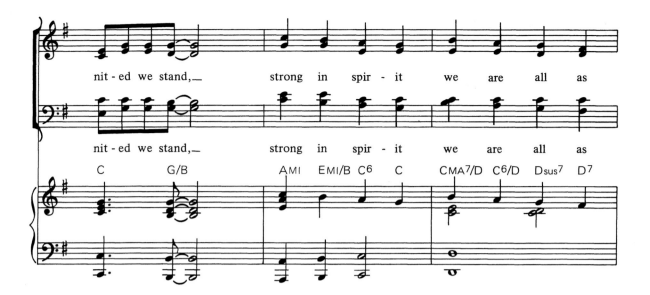

nit - ed we stand,___ strong in spir - it we are all as

nit - ed we stand,___ strong in spir - it we are all as

C   G/B   AMI EMI/B C6 C   CMA7/D C6/D Dsus7 D7

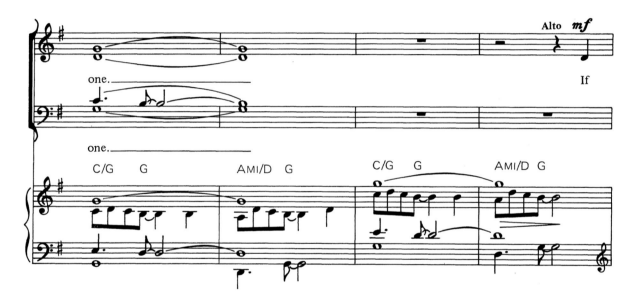

Alto *mf*

one.___

If

one.___

C/G G   AMI/D G   C/G G   AMI/D G

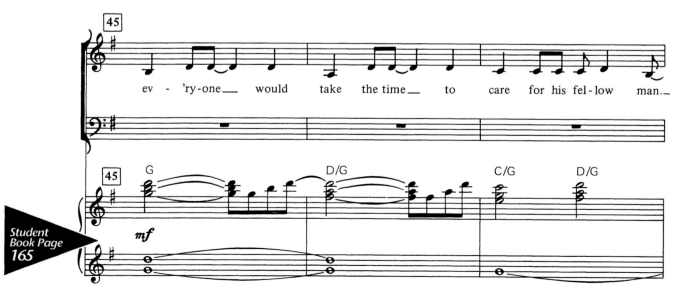

45

ev - 'ry-one___ would take the time___ to care for his fel - low man.___

45 G   D/G   C/G   D/G

mf

204

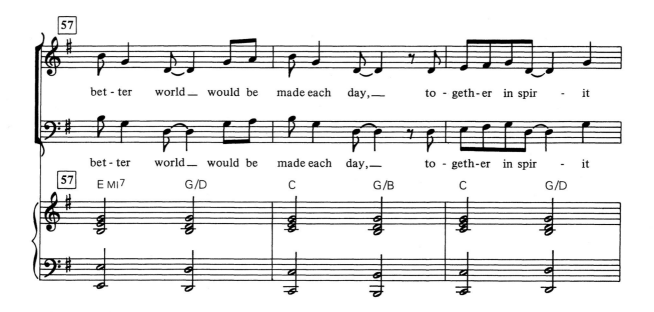

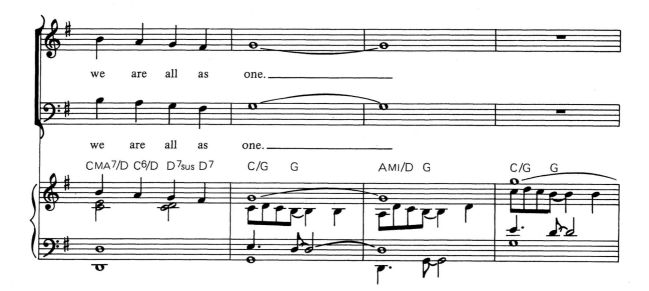

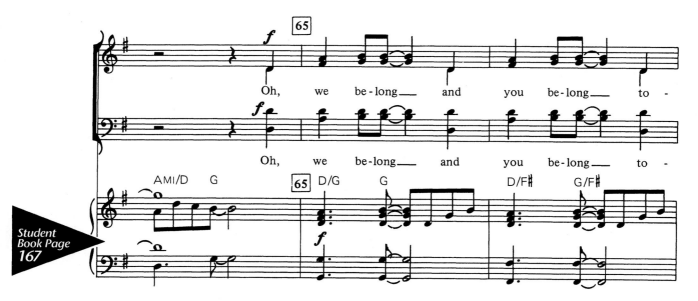

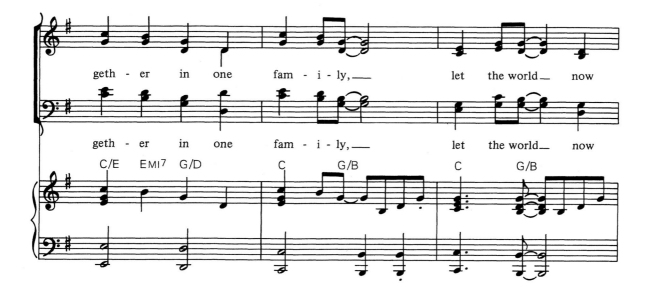

geth - er in one fam - i - ly, ___ let the world ___ now

geth - er in one fam - i - ly, ___ let the world ___ now

C/E EMI7 G/D   C   G/B   C   G/B

cel - e - brate ___ and live in per - fect har - mo-ny. ___

cel - e - brate ___ and live in per - fect har - mo-ny. ___

C   G/B   AMI EMI/B C6 C   D6   D

73

We be-long ___ and you be-long ___ to - geth - er in one

We be-long ___ and you be-long ___ to - geth - er in one

73
D/G   G   D/F#   G   C/E EMI7 G/D

Student
Book Page
168

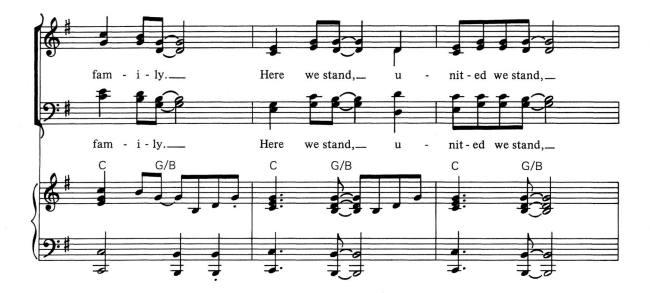

fam - i - ly.___ Here we stand,___ u - nit - ed we stand,___

C   G/B   C   G/B   C   G/B

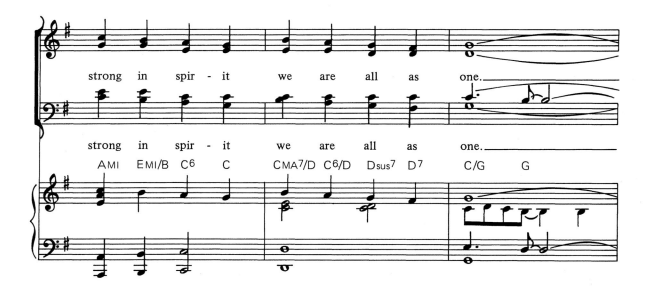

strong in spir - it we are all as one.___

AMI EMI/B C⁶ C   CMA⁷/D C⁶/D Dsus⁷ D⁷ C/G   G

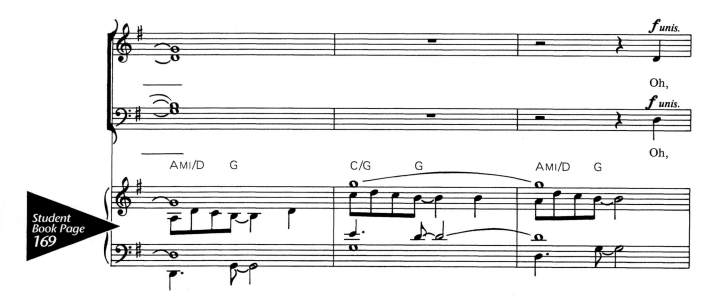

f unis.

Oh,

f unis.

Oh,

AMI/D G   C/G G   AMI/D G

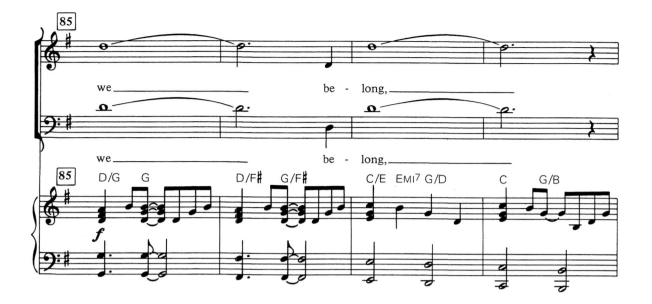

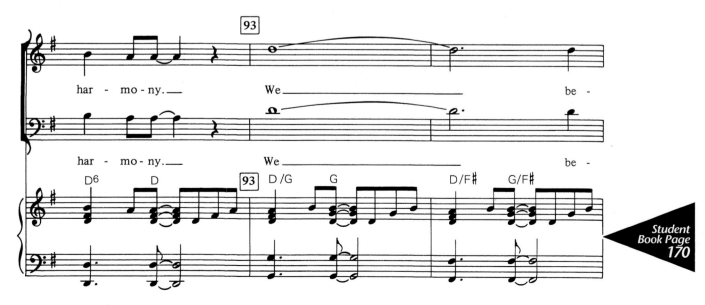

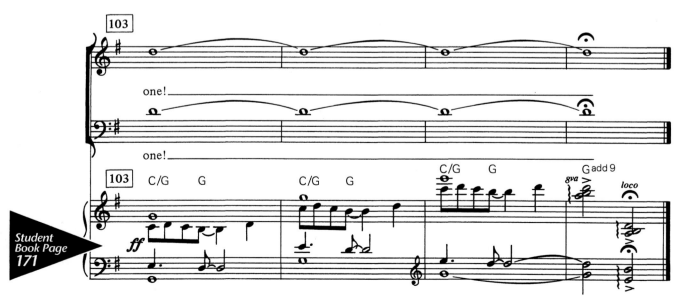

GLOSSARY

a cappella [It.] (ah-kah-PEH-lah) - Singing without instrumental accompaniment.

accelerando (*accel.*) [It.] (ahk-chel-leh-RAHN-doh) - Becoming faster; a gradual increase in tempo.

accent (>) - Stress or emphasize a note (or chord) over others around it. Accents occur by singing the note louder or stressing the beginning consonant or vowel.

accidentals - Symbols that move the pitch up or down a half step.

- sharp (♯) - raises the pitch one half step.
- flat (♭) - lowers the pitch one half step.
- natural (♮) - cancels a previous *sharp* or *flat*. (When it cancels a flat, the pitch is raised one half step; when it cancels a sharp, the pitch is lowered one half step).

Accidentals affect all notes of the same pitch that follow the accidental within the same measure, or if an altered note is *tied* over a *barline*.

adagio [It.] (ah-DAH-jee-oh) - Tempo marking indicating slow.

al fine [It.] (ahl FEE-neh) - To ending. An indicator following *D.C.* or *D.S.* From the Latin *finis*, "to finish."

allargando (*allarg.*) [It.] (ahl-lar-GAHN-doh) - Broadening, becoming slower, sometimes with an accompanying *crescendo*.

allegro [It.] (ah-LEH-groh) - Tempo marking indicating fast.

alto - A treble voice that is lower than the *soprano*, usually written in the *treble clef*.

andante [It.] (ahn-DAHN-teh) - Tempo marking indicating medium or "walking" tempo.

animato [It.] (ah-nee-MAH-toh) - Style marking meaning animated.

arranger - The person who takes an already existing composition and reorganizes it to fit a new instrumentation or voicing.

articulation - The clear pronunciation of text using the lips, teeth, and tongue. The singer must attack consonants crisply and use proper vowel formation.

a tempo - Return to the original tempo.

balletto [It.] (bah-LEH-toh) - A 16th century vocal composition with dance-rhythms and often phrases of nonsense syllables like "fa-la-la." Giovanni Gastoldi wrote the earliest known collection of balletti.

bar - See *measure*.

barline - A vertical line that divides the staff into smaller sections called measures. A double barline indicates the end of a section or piece of music.

Barline   Double Barline

Baroque Period (ca. 1600-1750) - (bah-ROHK) The period in Western music history that extended from 1600 to about 1750; also the musical styles of that period. The style features of most Baroque music are frequent use of *polyphony*; fast, motor-like rhythms; and use of the chorale. Some famous Baroque composers were J.S. Bach, G.F. Handel, and Antonio Vivaldi.

bass - A male voice written in *bass clef* that is lower than a *tenor* voice.

bass clef - The symbol at the beginning of the staff used for lower voices and instruments, and the piano left hand. It generally refers to pitches lower than *middle C*. The two dots are on either side of F, so it is often referred to as the F clef.

beat - The unit of recurring pulse in music.

breath mark (,) - An indicator within a phrase or melody where the musician should breathe. See also *no breath* and *phrase marking*.

caesura (//) [Fr.] (seh-SHOO-rah) - A break or pause between two musical phrases. Also called a *break*.

call and response - Alternation between two performers or groups of performers. Often used in *spirituals*, this technique begins with a leader (or group) singing a phrase followed by a response of the same phrase (or continuation of the phrase) by a second group.

canon - A musical form in which a melody in one part is followed a short time later by other parts performing the same melody. Canons are sometimes called *rounds*.

cantata [It.] (cahn-TAH-tah) - A large work (originally sacred) involving solos, chorus, organ, and occasionally orchestra. The cantata tells a story through text and music. Johann Sebastian Bach wrote a cantata for each Sunday of the church year.

chantey - A song sung by sailors in rhythm with their work.

chord - Three or more pitches sounding at the same time or in succession as in a broken chord. See also *interval*.

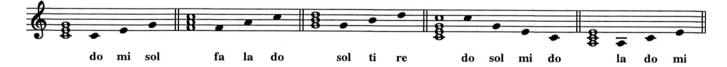

chromatic - Moving up or down by half steps, often outside of the key. Also the name of a scale composed entirely of half steps (all twelve pitches within an *octave*). The chromatic scale is distinct from the *diatonic* scale.

Classical Period (ca. 1750-1835) - The period in Western music history began in Italy in 1750 and continued until about 1825. Music of the Classical Period emphasized balance of phrase and structure. Ludwig von Beethoven, W.A. Mozart, and Joseph Haydn were famous composers from the Classical Period.

clef - The symbol at the beginning of the staff that identifies a set of pitches. See also *bass clef* and *treble clef*.

coda (⊕) [It.] (COH-dah) - Ending. A concluding portion of a composition.

common time (C) - Another name for the meter 4/4. See also *cut time*.

composer - The writer or creator of a song or musical composition. See also *arranger*.

compound meter - Meters which have a multiple of 3 such as 6 or 9 (but not 3 itself). Compound meter reflects the note that receives the division unlike *simple meter*. (Ex. 6/8 = six divisions to the beat in two groups of three where the eighth note receives one division). An exception to the compound meter rule is when the music occurs at a slow tempo, then the music is felt in beats rather than divisions. See also *meter* and *time signature*.

con [It.] (kawn) - With.

crescendo (*cresc.* or ———◁) [It.] (kreh-SHEN-doh) - Gradually growing louder. The opposite of *decrescendo*.

cued notes - Smaller notes indicating either *optional harmony* or notes from another voice part.

cut time (¢) - 2/2 time, the half note gets the beat.

da capo (D.C.) [It.] (dah KAH-poh) - Repeat from the beginning. See also *dal segno* and *al fine*.

dal segno (D.S.) [It.] (dahl SAYN-yoh) - Go back to the sign (𝄋) and repeat.

D.C. al fine [It.] - Repeat from the beginning to *fine* or end. See also *da capo* and *al fine*.

decrescendo (*decresc.* or ▷———) [It.] (deh-kreh-SHEN-doh) - Gradually growing softer. The opposite of *crescendo*. See also *diminuendo*.

descant - A high ornamental voice part often lying above the melody.

diatonic - Step by step movement within a regular scale (any key). A combination of the seven whole and half steps (of different pitch names) in a key. Distinct from *chromatic*.

diminuendo (*dim.*) [It.] (dih-min-new-EN-doh) - Gradually growing softer. See also *decrescendo*.

diphthong (DIPH-thong) - A combination of two vowel sounds consisting of a primary vowel sound and a secondary vowel sound. The secondary vowel sound is (usually) at the very end of the diphthong. (Ex. The word "I" is really a diphthong using an "ah" and an "ee." The "ee" is a very brief sound at the end of the word.)

divisi (div.) [It.] (dee-VEE-see) - Divide; the parts divide.

dolce [It.] (DOHL-cheh) - Sweetly; usually soft as well.

dotted barline - A "helper" *barline* in songs with unusual *time signatures* such as 5/8 and 7/8. The dotted barline helps divide the measure into two or more divisions of *triple* or *duple* beat groups.

downbeat - The accented first beat of the measure.

D.S. al Coda [It.] (ahl KOH-dah) - Repeat from the sign (𝄋) and sing the *coda* when you see the symbol (⊕).

D.S. al fine [It.] (ahl FEE-neh) - Repeat from the sign (𝄋) to *fine* or ending.

duple - Any *time signature* or group of beats that is a multiple of 2.

dynamic - The loudness or softness of a line of music. Dynamic changes may occur frequently within a composition.

endings - ⌐1.¬ ⌐2.¬ (First and second endings) Alternate endings to a repeated section.

enharmonic - Identical tones which are named and written differently. For instance, F-sharp and G-flat are the same note, they are "enharmonic" with each other.

ensemble - A group of musicians, (instrumentalists, singers, or some combination) who perform together.

fermata (⌒) [It.] (fur-MAH-tah) - Hold the indicated note (or rest) for longer than its value; the length is left up to the interpretation of the director or the performer.

fine [It.] (FEE-neh) - Ending. From the Latin *finis*, "to finish."

flat (♭) -An *accidental* that lowers the pitch of a note one half step. Flat also refers to faulty intonation when the notes are sung or played sightly under the correct pitch.

forte (*f*) [It.] (FOR-teh) - Loud.

fortissimo (*ff*) [It.] (for-TEE-see-moh) - Very loud.

freely - A style marking permitting liberties with tempo, dynamics, and style. *Rubato* may also be incorporated.

grand staff - A grouping of two staves.

half step - The smallest distance (or *interval*) between two notes on a keyboard. Shown symbolically (v). The *chromatic* scale is composed entirely of half steps.

half time - See *cut time.*

harmonic interval - *Intervals* played simultaneously.

harmony - Two or more musical tones sounding simultaneously.

hemiola [Gr.] (hee-mee-OH-lah) - A unique rhythmical device in which the beat of a *triple meter* has the feeling of *duple meter* (or the reverse) regardless of *barlines* and *time signatures*. This is accomplished through *ties* and/or *accent* placement.

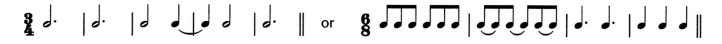

homophony [Gr.] (haw-MAW-faw-nee) - Music in which melodic interest is concentrated in one voice part and may have subordinate accompaniment (distinct from *polyphony* in which all voice parts are equal). Homophony is also music which consists of two or more voice parts with similar or identical rhythms. From the Greek words meaning "same sounds," homophony could be described as being "hymn-style."

hushed - A style marking indicating a soft, whispered tone.

interval - The distance between two pitches.

intonation - Accuracy of pitch.

key - The organization of tonality around a single pitch (*key-note*). See also *key-note* and *key signature*.

key-note - The pitch which is the tonal center of a key. The first tone (note) of a scale. It is also called the *tonic*. A key is named after the key-note; for example in the key of A-flat, A-flat is the key-note. See also *key* and *key signature*.

key signature - The group of *sharps* or *flats* at the beginning of a staff which combine to indicate the locations of the key-note and configuration of the *scale*. If there are no sharps or flats, the key is automatically C major or A minor.

 B♭ major or G minor

legato [It.] (leh-GAH-toh) - Smooth and connected. Opposite of *staccato*.

ledger lines (or leger lines) - The short lines used to extend the lines and spaces of the *staff*.

leggiero [It.] (leh-JEE-roh) - Light articulation; sometimes non-*legato*.

macaronic text - Text in which two languages are used (usually Latin and one other language).

madrigal - A kind of 16th century Italian composition based on secular poetry. Madrigals were popular into the 17th century.

maestoso [It.] (mah-ee-STOH-soh) - Majestic.

major key/scale/mode - A specific arrangement of whole steps and half steps in the following order:

Letter Names:	G	A	B	C	D	E	F♯	G
Moveable Do:	do	re	mi	fa	sol	la	ti	do
Fixed Do:	sol	la	ti	do	re	mi	fi	sol
Numbers:	1	2	3	4	5	6	7	1

See also *minor key/scale/mode*.

marcato [It.] (mahr-KAH-toh) - Marked or stressed, march-like.

mass - The central religious service of the Roman Catholic Church. It consists of several sections divided into two groups: Proper of the Mass (text changes for every day) and Ordinary of the Mass (text stays the same in every mass). Between the years 1400 and 1600 the mass assumed its present form consisting of the Kyrie, Gloria, Credo, Sanctus, and Agnus Dei. It may include chants, hymns, and psalms as well. The mass also developed into large musical works for chorus, soloists, and even orchestra.

measure - A group of beats divided by *barlines*. Measures are sometimes called *bars*. The first beat of each measure is usually accented.

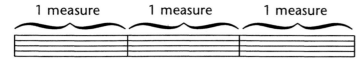

melisma - Long groups of notes sung on one syllable of text.

melodic interval - Notes that comprise an *interval* played in succession.

melody - A succession of musical tones; also the predominant line in a song.

meter - A form of rhythmic organization (grouping of beats). The kind of meter designated by the *time signature*. See also *simple* and *compound meters*.

meter signature - See *time signature*.

metronome marking - A marking which appears over the top staff of music which indicates the kind of note which will get the beat, and the number of beats per minute as measured by a metronome. It reveals the *tempo*. (Ex. (♩= 100)).

mezzo forte (*mf*) [It.] (MEH-tsoh FOR-teh) - Medium loud.

mezzo piano (*mp*) [It.] (MEH-tsoh pee-AH-noh) - Medium soft.

middle C - The C which is located closest to the middle of the piano keyboard. Middle C can be written in either the *treble* or *bass clef*.

minor key/scale/mode - A specific arrangement of whole steps and half steps in the following order:

Letter Names:	D	E	F	G	A	Bb	C	D
Moveable La:	la	ti	do	re	mi	fa	sol	la
Fixed La:	re	mi	fa	sol	la	te	do	re
Numbers:	1	2	3	4	5	6	7	1

See also *major key/scale/mode.*

mixed meter - Frequently changing meters or *time signatures* within a piece of music.

modulation - Changing keys within a song. Adjust to the *key signature*, the *key-note*, and proceed.

molto [It.] (MOHL-toh) - Much, very. (Ex. molto rit. = greatly slowing).

monophony - Music which consists of a single melody. This earliest form of composition is from the Greek words meaning "one sound." Chant or plainsong is monophony.

mosso [It.] (MOH-soh) - Moved, agitated.

mysterioso [It.] (mih-steer-ee-OH-soh) - A style marking indicating a mysterious or haunting mood.

natural (♮) - Cancels a previous *sharp* (♯) or *flat* (♭). (When it cancels a flat, the pitch is raised one half step; when it cancels a sharp, the pitch is lowered one half step.)

no breath (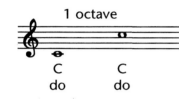 **or N.B.)** - An indication by either the *composer/arranger* or the editor of where *not* to breathe in a line of music. See also *phrase marking*.

notation - All written notes and symbols which are used to represent music.

octave - The *interval* between two notes of the same name. Octaves can be indicated within a score using ‹8va› (octave above) and ‹8vb› (octave below).

1 octave
C   C
do   do

ostinato [It.] (ah-stee-NAH-toh) - A repeated pattern used as a harmonic basis.

optional divisi (opt. div.) [It.] (dee-VEE-see) - The part splits into optional harmony. The smaller sized *cued notes* indicate the optional notes to be used.

phrase marking (⌒ **)** - An indication by either the *composer* or the *arranger* as to the length of a line of music or melody. This marking often means that the musician is not to breathe during its duration. See also *no breath*.

piano (*p*) [It.] (pee-AH-noh) - Soft.

pianissimo (*pp*) [It.] (pee-ah-NEE-see-moh) - Very soft.

pick-up - An incomplete measure at the beginning of a song or phrase.

pitch - The highness or lowness of musical sounds.

più [It.] (pew) - More. (Ex. più forte or più mosso allegro).

poco [It.] (POH-koh) - Little. (Ex. poco cresc. = a little crescendo).

poco a poco [It.] (POH-koh ah POH-koh) - Little by little (Ex. poco a poco cresc. = increase in volume, little by little).

polyphony [Gr.] (pahw-LIH-fahw-nee) - Music which consist of two or more independent melodies which combine to create simultaneous voice parts with different rhythms. Polyphony often involves contrasting dynamics and imitation from part to part. From the Greek words meaning "many sounds," polyphony is sometimes called counterpoint.

presto [It.] (PREH-stoh) - Very fast.

rallentando (*rall.*) [It.] (rahl-en-TAHN-doh) - Gradually slower. See also *ritardando*.

relative major/minor - Major and minor tonalities which share the same *key signature*.

G major   E minor

Renaissance Period (ca. 1450-1600) (REHN-neh-sahns) - A period in the Western world following the Middle Ages. Renaissance means "rebirth" and was a celebration of entrance into the modern age of thought and invention. In music it was a period of great advancement in notation and compositional ideas. *Polyphony* was developing and the *madrigal* became popular. Orlando di Lasso, Giovanni da Palestrina, Tomás Luis de Victoria, and Josquin Des Prez were some of the more famous Renaissance composers.

repeat sign (‖: :‖) - Repeat the section. If the repeat sign is omitted, go back to the beginning. See also *endings*.

resolution (res.) - A progression from a dissonant tone or harmony to a consonant harmony. (Usually approached by step.) See also *suspension*.

rhythm - The organization of non-pitched sounds in time. Rhythm encompasses note and rest duration as well as *meters*, *tempos*, and their relationships.

ritardando (*rit.*) [It.] (ree-tahr-DAHN-doh) - Gradually slower. See also *rallentando*.

Romantic Period (ca. 1825-1900) - A period in 19th century Western art, literature, and music that lasted into the early 20th century. In music, as well as the other areas, Romanticism focused on the emotion of art. Works from this period emphasized the emotional effect music has on the listener through dynamic contrasts and different ways of changing the "mood." Opera flourished as well as chamber music. Some famous Romantic composers are Franz Schubert, Frederick Chopin, Hector Berlioz, Johannes Brahms, and Richard Wagner.

root tone - The lowest note of a *triad* in its original position; the note on which the chord is built and named.

round - see *canon*.

rubato [It.] (roo-BAH-toh) - The tempo is free, left up to the interpretation of the director or performer.

scale - An inventory or collection of pitches. The word "scale" (from the Italian *scala*) means ladder. Thus, many musical scales are a succession of pitches higher and lower.

do   re   mi   fa   sol   la   ti   do   la   ti   do   re   mi   fa   sol   la
G major   E minor

score - The arrangement of a group of vocal and instrumental staffs which all sound at the same time.

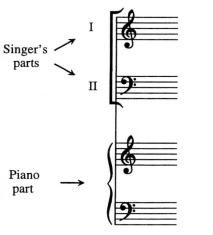

sempre [It.] (SEHM-preh) - Always , continually. (Ex. sempre forte = always loud)

sequence - The successive repetition of a short melodic idea at different pitch levels.

sharp (♯) - An *accidental* that raises the pitch of a note one half step. Also, faulty intonation in which the note is sung slightly above the correct pitch.

sign (𝄋 **or Segno**) [It.] (SAYN-yoh) - A symbol that marks the place in music where the musician is to skip back to from the *dal Segno* (*D.S.*).

simile (*sim.*) [It.] - (SIM-eh-lee) Continue the same way.

simple meter - Meters which are based upon the note which receives the beat. (Ex. 4/4 or **C** is based upon the quarter note receiving the beat.)

skip - The melodic movement of one note to another in *intervals* larger than a step.

slide ( ) - To approach a note from underneath the designated pitch and "slide" up to the correct pitch. Slides often appear in jazz, pop tunes, and *spirituals*.

slur ( ) - A curved line placed above or below a group of notes to indicate that they are to be sung on the same text syllable. Slurs are also used in instrumental music to indicate that the group of notes should be performed *legato* (smoothly connected).

solfège [Fr.] (SOHL-fehj) - The study of sight-singing using pitch syllables (do re mi, etc.).

soprano - The highest treble voice, usually written in *treble clef.*

spirito [It.] (SPEE-ree-toh) - Spirit.

spiritual - Religious folk songs of African American origin associated with work, recreation, or religious gatherings. They developed prior to the Civil War and are still influential today. They have a strong rhythmic character and are often structured in *call and response*.

219

spoken - Reciting text with the speaking voice rather than singing the designated line. Often indicated with 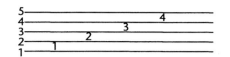 instead of notes.

staccato (◦) [It.] (stah-KAH-toh -) Short, separated notes. Opposite of *legato*.

staff - The five horizontal parallel lines and four spaces between them on which notes are placed to show *pitch*.

The lines and spaces are numbered from the bottom up.

step - Melodic movement from one note to the next higher or lower *scale* degree.

style marking - An indicator at the beginning of a song or section of song which tells the musician in general what style the music should be performed. (Ex. *freely* or *animato*)

subito (*sub.*) [It.] (SOO-bee-toh) - Suddenly. (Ex. sub. piano = suddenly soft)

suspension (sus.) - The sustaining or "suspending" of a pitch from a consonant chord into a dissonant chord often using a *tie*. The resulting dissonant chord then *resolves* to a consonant chord. The musical effect is one of tension and release. See also *resolution*.

swing - A change in interpretation of eighth note durations in some music (often jazz and blues). Groups of two eighth notes are no longer sung evenly, instead they are performed like part of a *triplet*. The eighth notes still appear. A swing style is usually indicated at the beginning of a song or section.

syllables - Names given to pitch units or rhythm units to aid in sight-reading.

syncopation - The use of *accents* and *ties* to create rhythmic interest. The result is a rhythmic pattern which stresses notes on the off beat. This technique is commonly found in *spirituals and jazz*.

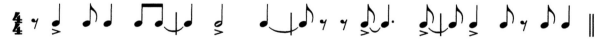

tempo - The speed of the beat.

tempo primo [It.] (TEHM-poh PREE-moh) - Return to the first (*primo*) tempo. See *Tempo I*.

tempo I - Return to the first tempo. Also called tempo primo.

tenor - A male voice written in *bass clef* or *treble clef*. It is lower than the *alto*, but higher than the *bass*.

tenuto (◦̄) [It.] (teh-NOO-toh) - A slight stress on the indicated note. The note is held for its full value.

texture - The interrelationship of the voices and/or instruments within a piece of music. *Monophonic, homophonic,* and *polyphonic* are all types of textures.

tie ( ) - A line connecting two or more notes of the same pitch so that their durations are their combined sum. Often occurring over *barlines*.

time signature - The symbol placed at the beginning of a composition or section to indicate its meter. This most often takes the form of a fraction (⁴⁄₄ or ³⁄₄), but may also involve a symbol as in the case of common time (**c**) and cut time (**¢**). The upper number indicates the number of beats in a measure and the lower number indicates which type of note receiving the beat. (An exception occurs in *compound meters*. See *compound meter* for an explanation.)

to coda - Go to the ⊕ .

tonality - The organization of *pitches* in a song in which a certain pitch (tone) is designated as the *key-note* or the note which is the tonal center of a *key*.

tone - A musical sound of definite pitch and quality.

tonic - The *key-note* of a key or scale.

tonic chord - The name given to the chord built on the *key-note* of the scale.

transpose - To rewrite or perform a song in a *key* other than the original.

treble clef - The symbol at the beginning of the staff used for higher voices and instruments, and the piano right hand. It generally refers to pitches higher then *middle C*. The curve is wrapped around the G, as a result it is also called the G clef.

triad - A special type of 3-note chord built in 3rds over a *root tone*.

trill (*tr* 〰〰) - Rapid alteration (within a key) between the marked note and the one above it.

triple - Any *time signature* or group of beats that is a multiple of 3.

triplet - A borrowed division of the beat where three notes of equal duration are to be sung in the time normally occupied by two notes of equal duration. Usually indicated with a 3.

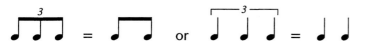

unison (unis.) - All parts singing the same notes at the same time, (or singing in *octaves*).

villancico [Sp.] (vee-yahn-SEE-koh or bee-yahn-SEE-koh) - A composition of Spanish origin from the 15th and 16th centuries. Similar to the *madrigal*, this type of work is based on secular poetry and is structured around the verses and refrains of its text.

vivace [It.] (vee-VAH-cheh) - Very fast.

whole step - The combination of two successive half steps. Shown symbolically (⊔).

BIBLIOGRAPHY

Alderson, Richard. *Complete Handbook of Voice Training*. West Nyack, New York: Parker Publishing Co., Inc., 1979.

Baker, Theodore, ed. *Schirmer Pronouncing Pocket Manual of Musical Terms*. 4th ed., rev. by Nicolas Slonimsky. New York: Schirmer Books, 1978.

___. *Baker's Biographical Dictionary of Musicians*. 6th ed., completely rev. by Nicolas Slonimsky. New York: Schirmer Books, 1978.

Bartle, Jean A. *Lifeline for Children's Choir Directors*. London: Oxford Press, 1988.

Bjorneberg, Paul, ed. *Exploring Careers in Music*. Reston, Virginia: Music Educators National Conference, 1990.

Claghorn, Charles Eugene. *Biographical Dictionary of American Music*. West Nyack, New York: Parker Publishing, Co., 1973.

Coffin, Berton. *Overtones of Bel Canto*. Metuchen, New Jersey: The Scarecrow Press, 1980.

Collins, Don L. *Teaching Choral Music*. Englewood Cliffs, New Jersey: Prentice-Hall, 1993.

Consortium of National Arts Education Associations. *National Standards for Arts Education: What Every Young American Should Know and Be Able to Do in the Arts*. Reston, Virginia: Music Educators National Conference, 1994.

Cooksey, John M. "The Development of a Contemporary, Eclectic Theory for the Training and Cultivation of the Junior High School Male Changing Voice." Parts 1-4. *Choral Journal* 18:2-5 (1977-78). (Note: These are four articles printed in a series.)

Decker, Harold A., and Julius Herford, eds. *Choral Conducting Symposium*. 2nd ed. Englewood Cliffs, New Jersey: Prentice Hall, Inc., 1988.

De Angelis, Michael. *The Correct Pronunciation of Latin According to Roman Usage*. St. Gregory Guild, Inc., 1965.

Downs, Philip G. *Classical Music: The Era of Haydn, Mozart, and Beethoven*. New York: W.W. Norton & Company, Inc., 1992.

Ehmann, Wilhelm, and Frauke Haasemann. *Voice Building for Choirs*. Chapel Hill, North Carolina: Hinshaw Music, Inc., 1982.

Ehret, Walter, and George K. Evans. *The International Book of Christmas Carols*. Englewood Cliffs, New Jersey: Prentice-Hall, 1963.

Ewen, David. *All the Years of American Popular Music*. Englewood Cliffs, New Jersey: Prentice-Hall, Inc., 1977.

___. *The Complete Book of Classical Music*. Englewood Cliffs, New Jersey: Prentice-Hall, Inc., 1966.

___. *The World of Twentieth Century Music*. Englewood Cliffs, New Jersey: Prentice-Hall, Inc., 1968.

Feitz, Leland. *Cripple Creek! A Quick History of the World's Greatest Gold Camp*. Colorado Springs, Colorado: Little London Press, 1967.

Gackle, Lynn. "The Adolescent Female Voice: Characteristics of Change and Stages of Development." *Choral Journal* 31(8)(1991): 17-25.

Grout, Donald J., and Claude V. Palisca. *A History of Western Music*. 4th ed. New York: W.W. Norton & Company, Inc., 1988.

Grun, Bernard. *The Timetables of History*. 3rd ed. New York: Simon & Schuster, 1991.

Haasemann, Frauke, and James M. Jordan. *Group Vocal Techniques*. Chapel Hill, North Carolina: Hinshaw Music Inc. 1991.

Hoffer, Charles R. *Teaching Music in the Secondary Schools*. 4th ed. Belmont, California: Wadsworth Publishing, Company, 1991.

Johnston, Richard. *Folk Songs North America Sings*. Toronto: E. C. Kerby, Ltd., 1984.

Kennedy, Michael. *The Concise Oxford Dictionary of Music*. 3rd ed. Oxford, England: Oxford University Press, 1980.

Lamb, Gordon H. *Choral Techniques*. 3rd ed. Dubuque, Iowa: Wm. C. Brown Company Publishers, 1988.

Lomax, Alan. *The Folk Songs of North America*. Garden City, New York: Doubleday & Company, Inc., 1975.

Marshall, Madeleine. *The Singer's Manual of English Diction*. New York: Schirmer Books, 1953.

May, Wiliiam V., and Craig Tolin. *Pronunciation Guide for Choral Literature: French, German, Hebrew, Italian, Latin, Spanish*. Reston, Virginia: Music Educators National Conference, 1987.

Music Educators National Conference, Committee on Standards. *Guidelines for Performances of School Music Groups: Expectations and Limitations*. Reston, Virginia: Music Educators National Conference, 1986.

Music Educators National Conference, Task Force on Choral Music Course of Study. *Teaching Choral Music: A Course of Study*. Reston, Virginia: Music Educators National Conference, 1991.

Morgan, Robert P. *Twentieth-Century Music: A History of Musical Style in Modern Europe and America*. New York: W.W. Norton & Company, Inc., 1991.

New York State School Music Association. *NYSSMA Manual: A Resource Manual of Graded Solo & Ensemble Music, Suitable for Contests and Festivals*. Westbury, New York: New York State School Music Association, 1991.

Palisca, Claude V., ed. *Norton Anthology of Western Music, Vol. I*. New York: W. W. Norton & Company, 1980.

Pfautsch, Lloyd. *English Diction for Singers*. New York: Lawson Gould, Inc., 1971.

Plantiga, Leon. *Romantic Music: A History of Musical Style in Nineteenth-Century Europe*. New York: W.W. Norton & Company, Inc., 1984.

Randel, Don M., ed. *The New Harvard Dictionary of Music*. Cambridge, Massachusetts: The Belknap Press of Harvard University Press, 1986.

Rao, Doreen. *We Will Sing: Choral Music Experience*. New York: Boosey & Hawkes, 1993.

___, ed. *Choral Music for Children: An Annotated List*. Reston, Virginia: Music Educators National Conference, 1990.

Robinson, Ray and Allen Winold. *The Choral Experience*. New York: Harper's College Press, 1976.

Roe, Paul F. *Choral Music Education*. 2nd ed. Englewood Cliffs, New Jersey: Prentice-Hall, Inc., 1983.

Runfola, Maria, ed. *Proceedings of the Symposium on the Male Adolescent Changing Voice*. Buffalo, New York: State University of New York at Buffalo Press, 1984.

Sandburg, Carl. *The American Songbag*. New York: Harcourt Brace Jovanovich, Inc., 1955.

Sadie, Stanley, ed. *The New Grove Dictionary of Music and Musicians*. Washington D.C.: Grove's Dictionaries of Music, 1980.

Shaw, Kirby. *Vocal Jazz Style*. 2nd ed. Milwaukee, Wisconsin: Hal Leonard Corporation, 1987.

Stanton, Royal. *Steps to Singing for Voice Classes*. 2nd ed. Belmont, California: Wadsworth Publishing Company, Inc., 1976.

Ulrich, Homer. *A Survey of Choral Music*. New York: Harcourt Brace Jovanovich, Inc., 1973.

University Interscholastic League. *Prescribed Music List for Bands, Orchestras and Choirs*. University Interscholastic League, 1991-1994.

Uris, Dorothy. *To Sing in English*. New York: Boosey and Hawkes, 1971.

Vennard, William. *Singing, the Mechanism and the Technique*. New York: Carl Fischer, 1988.

Wall, Joan Robert Caldwell, Tracy Gavilanes, and Sheila Allen. *Diction for Singers: A Concise Reference for English, Italian, Latin, German, French, and Spanish Pronunciation*. Dallas: PST ...Inc., 1990.

Young, Carlton R. *Companion to the United Methodist Hymnal*. Nashvillle, Tennessee: Abingdon Press, 1993.

RECOMMENDED VIDEOS

Archibeque, Charlene, *Daily Workout for a Beautiful Voice: Featuring Charlotte Adams.* Santa Barbara, California: Santa Barbara Music Publishing.

Ehly, Eph. *Choral Singing Style.* Milwaukee, Wisconsin: Hal Leonard Corporation.

___. *Excellence in Conducting "The Natural Approach."* Milwaukee, Wisconsin: Hal Leonard Corporation.

___. *Positive Motivation for the Choral Rehearsal.* Milwaukee, Wisconsin: Hal Leonard Corporation.

___. *Tuning the Choir.* Milwaukee, Wisconsin: Hal Leonard Corporation.

Hassemann, Frauke, and James Jordan. *Group Vocal Technique.* Chapel Hill, North Carolina: Hinshaw Music.

Jacobson, John. *John Jacobson's Riser Choreography.* Milwaukee, Wisconsin: Hal Leonard Corporation.

Nelson, Charles, Austin King, and Jon Ashby. *The Voice: Three Professionals Discuss the Function, Abuses and Care of the Most Important Instrument of Communication.* Abilene, Texas: Voice Institute of West Texas at Abilene Christian University.

Wall, Joan, and Robert Caldwell. *The Singer's Voice: Breath.* Dallas, Texas: Pst...Inc.

___. *The Singer's Voice: Vocal Folds.* Dallas, Texas: Pst...Inc.

___. *The Singer's Voice: Vocal Tract.* Dallas, Texas: Pst...Inc.

___. *The Singer's Voice: Acoustics.* Dallas, Texas: Pst...Inc.

ABOUT THE AUTHORS

JANICE KILLIAN received degrees from the University of Kansas, University of Connecticut, and earned her Ph.D. from the University of Texas-Austin. Throughout her career she has focused primarily on the junior high choral experience, but her teaching background includes K-12 public school experiences in Kansas, Connecticut, Minnesota, and Texas, as well as higher education experience at the State University of New York at Buffalo. Currently Dr. Killian is a member of the music faculty at Texas Woman's University in Denton, Texas, where her duties include directing a choral ensemble, teaching graduate and undergraduate music education classes, and conducting music education research.

MICHAEL O'HERN has been the choral director at Lake Highlands Junior High in Richardson, Texas, since the fall of 1982. A graduate of West Texas State University, Mr. O'Hern has completed graduate work at East Texas State University and The University of Texas at Arlington. A former RISE Foundation "Teacher of the Year" for the Richardson School District, Mr. O'Hern is often called upon to serve as a clinician and adjudicator throughout Texas. He serves as a soloist throughout the Dallas area. His choirs have won numerous awards at local, state, and national competitions. The Lake Highlands Junior High Chorale performed for the Texas Music Educators Convention in 1989 and 1994.

LINDA RANN has earned undergraduate and graduate degrees in Music Education from Louisiana State University in Baton Rouge with additional studies at Sam Houston State University, Texas Woman's University, University of North Texas, and Westminster Choir College. She is currently choral director at Dan Long Middle School in the Carrollton-Farmers Branch I.S.D., Carrollton, Texas, where her choirs are consistent sweepstakes winners. With over twenty years of public school teaching experience in elementary and middle school vocal music, Mrs. Rann is a frequent choral clinician and adjudicator. She has presented workshops nationally in the areas of middle school choral music and assessment in the performing arts.